And you who seek to know me, know that your seeking
and yearning will avail you not, unless you know the mystery:
for if that which you seek you find not within yourself,
you will never find it without.

THE CHARGE OF THE GODDESS

About the Author

Ellen Dugan, also known as the Garden Witch, is a psychic-clairvoyant who lives in Missouri with her husband and three children. A practicing Witch for over twenty-four years, Ellen also has many years of nursery and garden center experience, including landscape and garden design. She received her Master Gardener status through the University of Missouri and her local county extension office. Look for other articles by Ellen in Llewellyn's annual *Magical Almanac*, *Wicca Almanac*, and *Herbal Almanac*. Visit her website at:

www.ellendugan.com

Ellen Dugan

Natural Witchery

Intuitive, Personal & Practical Magick

INCLUDES BOOK OF WITCHERY

Llewellyn Publications
Woodbury, Minnesota

FIRST EDITION
Seventh Printing, 2014

Book design and editing by Rebecca Zins
Cover design by Lisa Novak
Cover images: PhotoDisc: Objects of Nature (acorn); Comstock: Patterns of Nature (leaf background)
Cover image photographer: Jack Hollingsworth/© Blend Images/Alamy

Cover model(s) used for illustrative purposes only
and may not endorse or represent the book's subject

Llewellyn is a registered trademark of Llewellyn Worldwide Ltd.

Library of Congress Cataloging-in-Publication Data

Dugan, Ellen, 1963–
Natural witchery : intuitive, personal & practical magick / Ellen Dugan. —1st ed.
   p.   cm.
Includes bibliographical references and index.
ISBN: 978-0-7387-0922-2
1. Magic. I. Title.
BF1611.D84 2007
133.4'3–dc22

2007004835

Llewellyn Worldwide does not participate in, endorse, or have any authority or responsibility concerning private business transactions between our authors and the public.

All mail addressed to the author is forwarded but the publisher cannot, unless specifically instructed by the author, give out an address or phone number.

Any Internet references contained in this work are current at publication time, but the publisher cannot guarantee that a specific location will continue to be maintained. Please refer to the publisher's website for links to authors' websites and other sources.

Llewellyn Publications
A Division of Llewellyn Worldwide Ltd.
2143 Wooddale Drive
Woodbury, MN 55125-2989
www.llewellyn.com

Printed in the United States of America

Contents

CHAPTER 4

PERSONAL MAGICKAL DEVELOPMENT, 83

CHAPTER 5

STARTING A CIRCLE, 101

CHAPTER 8
SPIRITUALITY AND PERSONAL ADVANCEMENT, 173

BOOK OF WITCHERY, 197

Contents

Acknowledgments

To my magickal family, the Members of Greenwood Circle. Thanks, girls, for the support and for all the fun and camaraderie. Each of you reminded me in your own way to take this book back to where I intended it to be all along.

To my husband, Ken, and our children, Kraig, Kyle, and Erin, who all managed to survive the writing process of yet another book. Thanks for being understanding when I was distracted and absent-minded while writing on the good, creative days and for making me laugh on those tough writing days.

With appreciation to my editor, Becky Zins, and to Nanette Peterson, for all their help and encouragement. Finally, a special thanks to Jen, who reminded me very eloquently that spirituality is the tool we use to rekindle the magick.

*We see our place in Nature, we see whence
we have come and where we are going,
and we see our relationship to the Cosmos,
and the whole of life opens up.*

DIONE FORTUNE

A Natural Witch

Where have you come from, and where are you going, my magickal friend? You are probably, like many of us, trying to sort out your place in the grand scheme of things. Important, personal questions—like what is my magickal style? What should I call myself? Am I eclectic or traditional? Do I want to stay solitary, or should I join a group? How can I make my craft practical and personal, as well as incorporate it into my daily life?—are some of the common issues you face.

Perhaps, with all these questions floating around inside your head, you are feeling a little frustrated. The enchanting things that once thrilled you have become commonplace, and you are struggling to go further, to advance your magickal practice and to grow. I invite you to take another look at the quote at the top of this page. Go ahead, read it out loud. When I came across this quote, I felt a jolt go all the way to my shoes. It made things fall into place for me, and I thought it was important to share this wisdom with you.

A common scenario for those of us who have been in the Craft for a good amount of time is trying to figure out just where we belong—realizing what exactly our relationship is with the divine and, after coming so far in our studies, deciding where we go next. So, here you stand at the crossroads in your life, and now it's up to you to choose which way you will travel onward.

Hmm … have you considered traveling the path of a natural Witch? It's the one over there. It looks less traveled, and the low tree branches are blocking your view. Take a few steps closer, and check it out. Pull back the draping branches, and you'll discover that this path has indeed been walked by many other Witches over the years. Certainly it looks quieter, but here, surrounded by the hushed sounds of nature, you have the opportunity to look within.

Practicing as a natural Witch is a very traditional role. It's my thought that the term "natural Witch" simply defines a type of person who quietly follows the ways of the early wise women and cunning men. In the old days, these wise folk were the magicians, mystics, and healers of their communities. This is where our folklore and traditions originated from, after all; the long-established ways of the wise ones are beautiful, elegant, and simple.

These original practitioners lived in harmony with the land. They worked their craft quietly, relying on their instincts and intuitions. Magick and spirituality was a part of their everyday life, for they were in tune with the tides and rhythms of nature and the movement of the animals. They hunted, grew their crops, raised their families, and practiced their craft naturally, with the four elements and simple, earthy, and practical supplies. They were the true natural practitioners.

Much to my surprise, the term "natural Witch" is a somewhat controversial one these days. Such a fuss over something that is, at its very heart, so simple. There are some folks who don't like the term—they think it's too fluffy-bunny—and others who embrace it wholeheartedly.

Some nice women that I met at a festival a few years ago actually asked me if it was okay to refer to themselves as "natural Witches." They were troubled because they had read online somewhere that it wasn't a politically correct title to call oneself.

So there we stood in the middle of a clearing, me in practical jean shorts and a T-shirt and they in flowing floral sarongs. I was surprised by the question, as we had all been chatting about herb gardening for a while, and I guess they felt that they had to work up to the question. At first, I almost giggled, thinking they were teasing me—until I took a good look at their faces and saw that they were very concerned and upset that they might be committing some type of horrific magickal faux pas.

My answer to them was that they should refer to themselves in whichever way they pleased—to go with whatever title or term seemed correct to them. When they asked how they would know for sure, I told them to listen to their hearts for that inner *click*, and to pay attention to their intuition for that sense of "rightness." If they felt that, then they would know.

Well, their reactions were beaming smiles all around, followed by a hug and a thank-you. And I will admit that I was surprised by their relief to have someone tell them it was okay and not to worry about titles and such. But they did make an impression on me, and for the rest of that festival I was very aware of how folks referred to themselves and their various traditions.

Is a Natural Witch Authentic?

A natural Witch claims the right to live as they choose. They grow in their craft and learn by trial and error. They work quietly with the four elements and natural spell ingredients, and they rely on personal study, their own common sense, and, of course, their intuition. These magickal practitioners answer to a tough ethical standard: their own conscience.

Here is a question for you to consider. What do you imagine really makes a Witch authentic? Is it lineage, tradition, or degrees? Or is it how the individual expresses themselves in the Craft and how they interact with the gods? Could it possibly be as simple as defining a natural Witch as a person who senses the spirit or the magick in all things?

Yes, it is just that simple, if the Witch is sincere.

A Witch naturally experiences and works with the psychic tides and energies of the moon. They explore the elemental strengths with their own personalities and work for wisdom and knowledge by tapping into the power and themes of the four seasons. They have a flair for ritual and know that spellcasting is, in essence, a reworking of fate. A natural Witch recognizes that the simple act of writing a spell, creating an herb-laden wreath, or placing crystals around a consecrated candle, if done with intention, can achieve wondrous results. And they know this because they have an awareness and appreciation of nature and a reverence for the intuitive and magickal energies present in all things.

So you just go right on ahead and take this opportunity to express yourself naturally through your magick. Enjoy the opportunity for personal magickal development. Create wonderful changes, and celebrate your right to grow and to become an adept practitioner. The idea behind natural witchery is that magick is an art. And all art is full of growth, discovery, personality, intuition, creation, and self-expression.

This is your time, and this is your own personal path to travel. So center your energy, and take a few quiet moments for preparation. When you feel ready, turn the page, and let's begin to walk this enchanting path together. Here, you will have the opportunity to learn more about yourself and your natural abilities, and discover how to conjure up your own individual brand of witchery and magick.

Enjoy the journey.

Chapter 1

*The most beautiful experience we can have is the
mysterious ... the fundamental emotion which stands
at the cradle of true art and true science.*

ALBERT EINSTEIN

The Natural Witch and Intuition

The natural Witch is often self-trained. These down-to-earth practitioners absolutely rely on study, personal judgment, and their intuition. It has often been said that a Witch never stops studying and learning. This statement is very true and at the heart of the natural Witch's craft. I find it interesting that if you look up the meaning of the word "craft" in *Webster's New Collegiate Dictionary,* you'll discover a most illuminating definition: Craft (n.) 1. Strength, skill. 2. Skill in planning, making, or executing. 3. An occupation or trade requiring manual dexterity or artistic skill.

Witchcraft is a craft. It requires hands-on practice as you study and learn to become proficient at it. And just like any other type of craft, it can take years to find your own style and to develop your own personal techniques. And if you remember nothing else, remember that. This is about exploring your magickal preferences and celebrating your magickal style.

I honestly don't care how Hannah the High Priestess does it three states over; I care about you and what *your* interests and talents are. For this is how you become an adept practitioner. You get in there, rely on your instincts, roll up your sleeves, study, experiment, and do the work. Welcome to a journey of self-discovery.

So what makes you *you*? Defining who we are is more than the size of clothing you wear or the color of your eyes and hair. Our individuality comes from a light that is inside of us: that divine spark we all carry. It's our insights, spirits, and personality. Trying to categorize Witches and magickal practitioners is a tough job. Sure, we all have our favorite ways to describe ourselves, but let's step outside of the box, shall we? Celebrating our diversity in the Craft is an amazingly wonderful thing.

We are *not* all the same—thank Goddess! We each have our own ideas and ways of practicing our craft. This should be celebrated, because that's what makes us powerful, our personality and our individuality. And don't you ever forget it.

If you'd like to celebrate your right to be a magickal individual who listens to their intuition and follows their heart in the Craft, you have come to the right place. If these qualities remind you of yourself, then a natural approach to witchery is a good place for you to hang your Witch's hat. In the past, I have explored magick in the garden, in the home, and on each and every day of the week. This time, I want to go a little deeper and discuss our spirituality and individuality and to focus on our intuitions.

Learning how to trust your intuition, instincts, and psychic impressions is a phenomenal way to boost the power of your natural magick. And before you start to argue, *everyone* has intuition and psychic abilities! It's simply up to the individual to look inside and to realize their own potential. Just as the Charge of the Goddess states, if you can't find what you're looking for within yourself, you'll never find it without.

Now is when you must search deep inside your psyche and learn to be comfortable with yourself. I promise if you have the courage to do that, then you can develop new skills and a sensitivity to the magick around you. You will comprehend how to influence your environment and how to live your magickal life to the fullest. Together, we will discover how taking the journey within makes us stronger, unique, and more adept practitioners of the Craft.

> *The more we know, the better our intuition.*
> CHRISTINA STEAD

INTUITION:
WHAT IT IS AND WHY IT IS IMPORTANT

Magick is not only about working in harmony with the four elements and the natural world, it also involves listening to your intuition. Intuition itself comes from the primitive part of our brains—the primal force called the survival instinct. This force communicates vital information from a different level of the consciousness, sometimes dramatically, sometimes mundanely. Intuition doesn't arrive with swirls of pixie dust and an enchanting chime of harp strings; it's simply always there.

Intuition may be defined as a quick and ready insight and immediate apprehension or cognition—the good old-fashioned "gut hunch." You just *know.* For example, parents are very intuitive. They usually instinctively know when one of their kids is up to something or if one of them is ill. How about that feeling in the pit of your stomach that makes you turn around just in time to yank your toddler away from the hot stove? Or the hunch that makes you change lanes while driving because another driver is making you nervous, just in time to see that driver cut someone else off? When you realize with a start that if you hadn't paid attention and followed that hunch, you could have been in an accident. *That's* your intuition.

Discovering your psychic abilities and working with your intuition is more simple than you think. It's easier to trust your instincts when you feel a Witch's connection to the natural world and the divine. This psychic ability is part of your genetic makeup, and it is a tool and an ally. Once you learn how to honor and tap into your intuition, your magick and your life improve for the better.

One theory I found is that *magickal experiences are intuitive experiences felt at the spiritual level.* When I uncovered this, I was thrilled. Intuition isn't just a psychic thing; it is so much more. This natural ability corresponds with the magickal trinity of the earth, sea, and sky. No fooling! Intuition is associated with three main levels of awareness: the physical level, your bodily sensations, which ties to the earth; the emotional level, your feelings, which corresponds to the element of water and the sea; and finally the mental level, images and ideas, which links the element of air and the sky.

Paying attention to and then acting on your intuition is a leap of faith. It is a daring thing to do. Everyone has some type of psychic ability, and intuition is one of the easiest psychic abilities to coax out. And I'm about to show you just how to go about it. In this chapter, we will take a look at the different types of psychic abilities and see how to identify and access them. Let's get better acquainted with intuition so we can incorporate this very personal and individual psychic power into your life and your magick.

*The psychic mind is both the key
and doorway to our magickal talents.*
CHRISTOPHER PENCZAK

PSYCHIC ABILITIES AND THE CRAFT

As magickal practitioners, it is well worth taking the time to explore our psychic abilities. Acquiring an understanding of what our individual gifts are and how they work will enable us to connect with the wisdom deep within our own souls. This makes perfect sense to me, as the word *psychic* originally comes from the Greek word *psyche*, meaning "soul." This chapter will help you identify and discover your own strengths, as well as present ideas for adding this soul-power to your magick.

Without a doubt, we all have psychic abilities of some sort. If you look up the term *psychic* today, it is typically used to describe a person who is sensitive to nonphysical or supernatural forces. Now, personally, I don't buy into the term *supernatural*. Intuition and psychic abilities are perfectly natural; there is nothing otherworldly about them. I think a better term is "unseen." These unseen forces are all around you, all the time. To sense them, you need only to open up your awareness and take your sensitivity to a whole new level. So, how do you start? By acknowledging your intuition. This act can open up a person to many new levels of consciousness.

You do have the right to follow and express your intuition. Intuition is sometimes called the sixth sense. The sixth sense is beyond the traditional five of hearing, sight, smell, taste, and touch. The sixth sense is an internal awareness and a sense of perception that is outside of the expected, everyday flow of physical impressions and thoughts. These intuitive messages can be subtle—you may not even realize they are there until you train yourself to pay attention. At other times, they may grab hold of you and not shake loose until you focus on what they are trying to tell you.

Some folks will experience intuition as a quick spark of inspiration or sense it as a strong "gut hunch." You know, that feeling you get down in your belly that tightens painfully until you pay attention? That's a gut hunch. Other people think of it as an inner voice that whispers to them, and some folks experience psychic abilities in full-color images and visions. It's also common to get a combination effect of several of the above. No matter how it manifests, intuition is a powerful guide and ally.

Well then, how do you get the psychic abilities to "turn on"? You start by testing yourself and then you practice and begin working out those psychic muscles. There are a few tips and tricks I have learned over the years, and these psychic exercises can help you trigger your extrasensory abilities. Everyone can benefit from these exercises, and besides that, they are a lot of fun to do. The reason for flexing these new mystical muscles is simple: the more you develop your psychic abilities, the clearer your own magickal path can become.

PSYCHIC EXERCISES

Light Up Those Chakras

The seven chakras are zones of energy. Picture them as glowing orbs of energy arranged in a line straight down the center of the body. The chakras are all the colors of the rainbow:

CHAKRA	LOCATION	COLOR
root chakra	base of spine	red
belly	abdomen	orange
solar plexus	beneath rib cage	yellow
heart	middle of chest	green
throat	hollow of throat	blue
third eye	middle of forehead	violet
crown	top of head	white

One of the basic steps to turning on your psychic abilities is to light up the chakras. By this, I mean you envision them as pulsing with bright, glowing colors.

Studying the energy centers of the body could fill up an entire book on its own, but we are going to keep this simple here. This is a visualization exercise that only takes about five minutes. It calls for you to picture the chakras as glowing orbs of energy, and then turn up their light, so you visualize them glowing brightly and pulsing with energy.

Begin by getting out paper and a pen so you can quickly write down your impressions when you are finished with the exercise. Set them in a handy spot nearby. You can start this exercise by sitting easily on the floor and resting your hands comfortably in your lap. Roll your head around gently, and stretch out your neck and shoulders. Close your eyes. (This act will force you to focus on your psychic impressions, not your physical ones.) Take a few deep, cleansing breaths, and ground and center yourself.

Now picture the root chakra that sits at the base of your spine. This orb of light is bright red. This chakra is known as the seat of power, and it is a place of raw energy and a grounding force. This chakra connects you to the physical world. Picture this ball of light as glowing with a vivid red and warm light.

Next move up to the belly chakra. This chakra center is between the base of the spine and your navel, in the abdomen area. This sphere of light is orange. This chakra is thought to influence your instincts, emotions, and personal power. This is the area where "gut hunches" begin. Light it up and see the orb as glowing a beautiful, bright orange. If you feel your belly clenching as you turn on this power area, take a deep breath, and try to relax those muscles. After a moment, go ahead and move on.

Now we go to the solar plexus. This is directly beneath the rib cage and above the navel. This orb is a brilliant yellow color, and as you focus on this area you may notice it tightening up as well. What do you sense when you focus on this psychic center? This is considered the "soul area," and your psychic intuition and personal power are linked to this region of the body, as is your magickal will. This is the energy center where psychic impressions physically gather. At this point of the body, you can literally feel the intuitive impressions tighten up your muscles. Give yourself a moment to experience the sensation, and gather any impressions as you light up this area.

Next, turn your focus to the heart chakra. It will be a gorgeous grass-green color, found right where you'd expect it—the middle of the chest. From this energy center, your emotions and love radiate out. Unconditional love and strong emotions come from this chakra. Light up this sphere and feel the sensation of perfect love and perfect trust spread out through your whole body. Enjoy this lovely sensation for a bit, and then move on to the next chakra.

The throat chakra is located at the hollow of the throat. This chakra is a stunning sapphire blue. Turn it on, and visualize it as glowing bright along with the other chakras. This chakra controls how we communicate with others and how well we listen. Psychic hearing is governed from this area. As you visualize this chakra expanding and lighting up, listen carefully and see what your inner voice has to say.

Next, shift your focus up to the middle of your forehead, the third eye area. This chakra is a gorgeous amethyst-violet color. This energy center is the point of your psychic vision and perception. Illuminate this orb of light. Take a moment to experience the difference in your awareness as you focus on the center of energy that clairvoyance (called psychic sight) comes from. Give yourself a short time, and "see" what you can perceive.

Lastly, shift your attention to the top of your head, called the crown. The crown chakra is a brilliant white, and this where we experience and sense the divine in our lives. Here is where you link to the God and Goddess, in everyday life and during magick. From this chakra, we experience divine love. Let this orb billow out in a dazzling white halo, and take a moment to experience the love of all of creation.

Now that all seven chakras are lit up and pulsing with positive energy, take a few moments and enjoy the experience. What sort of psychic impressions are you gathering? Does one part of your body feel more "turned up" than the others? Focus on it, and ask yourself what you need to know. Don't think this to death; just see what you feel.

After a little while, turn down the brightness of the chakras. I like to picture a dimmer switch that I turn so the light gets softer. If it will help, pantomime the action of turning the switch down in a counterclockwise turn. If you notice one of the chakras is still bigger than the others or you have a tightening in one part of your body, take a deep breath, and make those muscles relax. If it helps, rub your hands over the area to help the muscles loosen up.

Then reach down to the floor directly in front of the base chakra and "zip" all the seven chakras closed. Raise your hand up in front of your body, in a straight line, and finish up as high as you can reach. No muss, no fuss. If you don't fling your arm around, it appears to the casual observer that you are merely stretching.

Ground and center, placing the palms of your hands flat on the ground. Hold that pose for a moment so that you may send any excess energy safely back into the earth and so you can pull up stabilizing energy from the earth as well, should you need it. Allow yourself to relax. Once you've done that, open your eyes, place your hands in a natural pose, and relax your posture. Take some time to jot down your impressions. Now that you've worked your way through this chakra exercise once, it only gets easier and quicker every time.

Receive Psychic Impressions as Easy as 1-2-3

If you want to receive psychic impressions swiftly, light up the chakras in order, just as in the first exercise. Then visualize the belly (orange), solar plexus (yellow), and third eye chakra (violet) spinning, expanding, and growing larger than the rest of the other chakras.

Hold this image in place for a few moments, and allow your perceptions to open up. Shift your attentions inward, and let your mind drift. What do you see, hear, or sense? What pops into your mind, and what causes you to have a physical reaction? By that I mean what impressions made your solar plexus or belly area tighten? After a few moments, turn the power down so all the chakras are the same size and intensity. Now zip them closed, and ground and center. Jot down your impressions. This 1-2-3 technique also comes in handy while working with any divinatory tool, such as the tarot or runes. It also helps when practicing psychometry, the psychic reading of objects by touch.

Find the Ace of Spades

This is a simple and fun way to warm up those psychic muscles. You will need one deck of regular playing cards. We'll work with playing cards here, because the images are bold and simple.

From the deck, pull out the ace of spades, the ace of hearts, and the ace of diamonds. Set the rest of the deck to the side. Now turn the three aces face down on a table, and mix them up well. Slide them back and forth in a circular motion over each other until you have no idea where the ace of spades is. Now, keeping the cards face down, line them up from left to right in a horizontal line in front of you. Now hold your hand over each card (without touching it), and guess where the ace of spades is. Think only about the suit of spades and the color black. Turn over your choice. How did you do?

With this exercise, you'll get to experiment and see how your intuition communicates with your conscious mind. You may hear an inner voice saying "this card." You may see the ace of spades in your mind's eye or the card may have a different "feel." Your solar plexus area may tighten up when you hold your hand over the correct card, or you may just know.

Try this exercise again, only this time touch the cards—see if that helps you find the ace of spades more easily. Then repeat for as long as you like. When finished, take a moment and write down how you intuited the correct card most often. Was it by listening to an inner voice? Did you sense the ace by touch? Or did you just instinctively know? Were you able to gather the information by a psychic visual impression or by tuning in to your solar plexus and following your gut hunch?

Now that you have your intuition turned on and are warming up and beginning to understand the process, let's take this neat little test and see where your psychic strengths lie.

The intellect has little to do on the road to discovery.
There comes a leap in consciousness, call it intuition
or what you will, the solution comes to you
and you don't know how or why.
The truly valuable thing is the intuition.
ALBERT EINSTEIN

DISCOVERING YOUR PSYCHIC ABILITIES

This quiz is divided up into five separate sections, each one representing a different psychic ability. This test uses a simple scoring method to give you an overall idea of where you stand in the range of psychic awareness. There are several questions in each section for you to read and then answer.

On a separate piece of paper, make five separate columns. Then write the topic heading of each section down, and add the numbers one through ten to each of the five sections. Read each numbered statement, and then write your yes or no answer down next to the corresponding number. Now, don't overthink these statements. If they honestly apply to you, then mark down "yes." If you start thinking, *Well, that sort of happened to me once, three years ago...*, then your answer is "no."

Clairaudient Quiz

1. While I am speaking to friends, I know what they are going to say—*before* they say it. (yes/no)

2. As I begin to fall asleep, I hear a voice call my name. (yes/no)

3. I often hear a friend or family member's voice in my head, even when they are not physically with me. (yes/no)

4. I hear key phrases or words in my mind that then play out immediately in real life. (yes/no)

5. When I am frightened or nervous about something, I hear a comforting and calming voice out of nowhere. (yes/no)

6. If I have a person's name stuck in my mind all day, I typically receive a "surprise" phone call or visit from them. (yes/no)

7. I will have a song spontaneously pop into my mind that then provides me with insights or information for a particular problem. (yes/no)

8. I always pay attention to my "inner voice." (yes/no)

9. I hear what other people are thinking. (yes/no)

10. It is essential to me to use the sounds of nature to unwind. (yes/no)

Clairvoyant Quiz

1. I regularly experience premonitions. (yes/no)

2. I feel that I can understand a pet or a loved one by looking into their eyes. (yes/no)

3. When I close my eyes, I can see actual images in my mind's eye. (yes/no)

4. I mistrust people who will not look me in the eyes or who look away while speaking to me. (yes/no)

5. I am attracted to light-filled rooms and bright, sunny colors. (yes/no)

6. Visualization techniques come easy for me. (yes/no)

7. While being taught something new, I do better by being shown as opposed to being told. (yes/no)

8. I have experienced a clairvoyant vision while I was awake and aware of my other surroundings. (yes/no)

9.   I insist upon having fancy props and elaborate altar setups while I work my magick. (yes/no)

10. I would describe myself as a visual type of person. (yes/no)

Precognitive Dreamer Quiz

1.   I always remember my dreams, both good and bad. (yes/no)

2.   I daydream in clear color pictures, complete with emotions and sound. (yes/no)

3.   As I drift off to sleep, unexplained images regularly pop into my head. (yes/no)

4.   I have precognitive dreams. (yes/no)

5.   My "psychic dreams" tend to be clearer, louder, and more vivid in detail. (yes/no)

6.   My dreams influence me during the daytime. (yes/no)

7.   I consider the bedroom my sanctuary. (yes/no)

8.   I enjoy working with symbolism as an integral part of my magickal practices. (yes/no)

9.   I enjoy solving puzzles or figuring out a mystery. (yes/no)

10. I have a vivid imagination. (yes/no)

Intuition or "Prophetic Knowing" Quiz

1. I have experienced a foreboding feeling (which may be described as a "sinking feeling in the pit of the stomach") about a person, place, or serious situation that then actually happens. (yes/no)

2. I tend to blurt out whatever comes to my mind without first thinking it over. (yes/no)

3. While driving, I often get a hunch about another driver—that they will do something dangerous or cause something to happen—and as I back off the other vehicle (just to be safe), it turns out I am correct. (yes/no)

4. I act on my "gut hunches," which is followed by a positive affirmation that it was the correct thing to have done. (yes/no)

5. I rarely worry because I "just know" things will turn out all right. (yes/no)

6. I let my instincts guide me while searching for a book or other new item to purchase. (yes/no)

7. I make major decisions quickly and correctly, as if by instinct. (yes/no)

8. I wake up right before the alarm clock goes off in the morning. (yes/no)

9. While working magick, I follow my instincts more than correspondences or guides. (yes/no)

10. I consider myself a quiet and contemplative type of person. (yes/no)

Empathy Quiz

1. As I enter a room, my first thoughts and impressions are usually about how the room "feels" to me. (yes/no)

2. I am easily influenced by other people's moods and emotions. (yes/no)

3. Being in a large crowd makes me feel physically uncomfortable and bombarded emotionally. (yes/no)

4. When I meet someone for the first time, I gather my impressions and assess them by how they make me feel, despite how they act. (yes/no)

5. I find the atmosphere in hospitals to be very uncomfortable, to the point where I feel physically ill. (yes/no)

6. I dislike and will try to avoid casual touching in social situations. (yes/no)

7. Having heirloom items or antiques in my home makes me feel uncomfortable because of the memories they carry. (yes/no)

8. I experience a feeling of "butterflies in the stomach" or a tightening of the solar plexus area when I am contemplating the possibility of an angry verbal confrontation or physical danger. (yes/no)

9. I am able to sense another person's emotional state by touching them. (yes/no)

10. I have my feelings hurt very easily and am quickly moved to tears. (yes/no)

Scoring the Test

Yes = 2 points

No = 0 points

Add up the scores and see which of the five areas you scored the highest in. Remember that you are going to have five separate scores. Use the following list to give yourself points for each of your answers in their respective categories. You may find there were a few sections that are very close in score—and if so, that's normal. We all use a mixture of intuitive abilities. The highest section that you scored in overall will show you where you natural psychic talents lie. Once you have checked out your scores, be sure to look at the following section, "Types of Psychic Abilities," where there is more detailed information about each of these five types of psychic abilities and also some insights as to why certain statements were on the quiz.

Section Scores

If you scored 0–8

My friend, you have work to do! You don't often pay attention to your psychic abilities, or perhaps you lack faith in them. You may sense *something* but are often at a loss as to how to tune in and understand the messages you receive. Now, it may simply be that this particular psychic ability is not your area of expertise, or you may need to open up your mind a bit and explore all the possibilities … time will tell. Work the exercises in this chapter and get those intuitive skills up and running!

If you scored 10–14

You are usually in touch with this psychic sense, even though you may not understand what is happening. Confidence is the keyword here. Keep track of your experiences, and document and validate them. In time, a pattern will emerge, and you will begin to comprehend your individual intuitive skills better than you ever imagined. Practice the Easy as 1-2-3 exercise on page 11, and try using your intuitive skills every day. Pick a favored divinatory tool and start working it!

If you scored 16–20

You are very aware that you have psychic abilities and rely on this particular talent often. While you may not have much practical experience combining them with magick, this shouldn't be hard for you to dive into. Read further along for more information on your particular area of skill, and then begin incorporating this intuitive side of your personality into your magick for some truly spectacular results.

Types of Psychic Abilities: How to Incorporate Them into Your Magick

Clairaudience

Clairaudience means "clear hearing": think of having psychic headphones on. This power is often centered at the base of the throat and up and around the lower sides of your head, around the ear area. Telepathy is associated with clairaudience, though telepaths often hear other people's voices or occasionally thoughts from another person's mind, or they simply hear what is not said—think of it as "hearing between the lines." This form of psychic information may seem a little creepy to some folks—and unless you are used to listening to your own inner monologue, it can be startling. With this type of psychic ability, the inner voice is usually a subtle and gentle nudge. If a feeling of nervousness or unease accompanies the "messages," then it may be very loud indeed, in order to get your attention.

Clairaudience involves the reception of extrasensory signals as a word, a sound, or even a song. Individuals who have this ability often try to talk themselves out of it. They are analytical thinkers and need to have clairaudience proved to them, and often. Since they pick up so much anyway, it's easy for them to tune it out and dismiss the impressions as coincidences. So how do you tell the difference between background noise and telepathic receptions? You pay attention to your body—it will be accompanied by a physical reaction. You get a rush, your face may feel warmer, your stomach muscles tighten, or your stomach "drops."

If you'd like to incorporate clairaudience into your magickal life, try asking yourself questions about planned spells or rituals, and then "listen" to your inner voice for the answers. Mantras and keywords will also work wonderfully for you, so choose a few positive ones and repeat them silently in your head when you need them. For a protection mantra, try this: "I stand in circles of light that nothing may cross." To boost your prosperity, try "I manifest prosperity in my life, in many ways and every single day." For self-healing, try "I manifest health, happiness, and strength for myself in the best possible way." For keywords, that's really easy. Just pick a few, such as "health," "success," "protection," or "wisdom"—you get the idea. Most folks who have strong clairaudient tendencies are quick thinkers, very direct, and are the no muss, no fuss type. So just keep it simple, and go with what works the best for you!

Clairvoyance

This term means "clear seeing." A clairvoyant sees images and pictures that may be symbolic, or they can be as intense as watching a miniature psychic movie scene inside your mind. These visual images are spiritual messages. This psychic talent is linked to the third eye chakra, where you receive the visual images from your mind's eye. To sharpen the images, try closing your eyes. This shifts your focus internally, and it has always done the trick for me.

There are a few different types of clairvoyant images. There can be a perceived picture, symbol, or an actual full-blown vision that lasts a moment or two. Here a psychic scene plays out in your mind, and these may be scenes from the past, present, or future. The environment you are in, the way people appear, the clothing, and the atmosphere will tip you off as to whether you are looking at the past, present, or future. Also ask yourself, slowly, "Am I seeing the past … present … or future?" Note which word causes a physical reaction, such as the solar plexus tightening. Whichever word causes a physical reaction, there's your answer.

You can incorporate clairvoyance into your magick quickly and easily. How? By using visualization. If you can't visualize, your spells will flop. Having a talent for receiving visual images and messages is like having the volume turned up on magick. You've got the power already, so just crank it and get ready to rock and roll. Envision your spell's outcome and see it as being manifested. Since you are already a visual type of person, this is a snap. Also, setting up and plotting out magick will be a breeze for you, as you have that mental picture to focus on.

On an interesting note, clairvoyance is linked to precognitive dreams. Since dreams are visual images, they do go hand in hand with clairvoyance. Chances are if you scored high in clairvoyance, then your precognitive dreams score is higher as well. So look over the next section, too, and see what you discover.

Precognitive Dreams

Precognitive dreams are usually full of symbols and emotions and have a vivid type of compelling force behind them. The easiest way to tell the difference between just a dream and a precognitive dream is the strength it carries behind it. These vivid dreams may jolt you awake or pop into your head as you lay in bed in the morning waking up. Also, you are usually present and have an active role in these dreams. Interpreting these dreams for yourself isn't difficult after all of the psychic senses are linked together. Look back at the dream, and ask yourself what you felt and what phrases popped into your mind. What do you *just know* about them?

Keeping a dream journal is one way to notice patterns and trends. For example, women may find that at different times of their monthly cycle they will have more vivid dreams. Also, the moon's cycles of waxing and waning may come into play. Keeping track of your dreams by noting the date and lunar phase—and of course writing them down—will offer you valuable clues. In your dream journal, you can jot down your dreams, and note any emotions or intuition that you feel as you transcribe the dream. In time, you will begin to notice patterns and symbols.

Intuition

Intuition is an immediate insight sensed as a cognition or apprehension: the "gut hunch." With this talent, you go with your gut—and follow your heart. This ability of intuition is also called "prophetic knowing." In the simplest terms, you *know*. The area of energy in the body that this ability comes from is the top of your head: the crown chakra. The great thing about intuition is that it's lightning fast. You don't have to examine the visions (as a clairvoyant would) or consider that internal voice and then interpret what the messages mean (as a clairaudient does). Again, you'll know. And that knowledge will ring clear for you, and you will recognize it to be true to your very soul. You will experience that sensation in your gut—a "hunch"—and you can then quickly follow your instincts.

Since intuitive folks are so sure, confident, quick, and clever, they are the least likely to worry and fret about the outcome of things. So if this is your area of power, use this to your advantage in magick. Get in there and follow your inner wisdom, and do the magickal work you know to be the best for yourself and the situation. Follow your instincts, and see where they lead you. Use your intuition as a quick, practical, and clever guide to magick and spellcraft.

Empathy

Empathy is also known as clairsentience. An empath is a person who can physically "tune in" to the emotional experience of a person or place. They sense attitudes, emotions, and sometimes physical ailments. It is believed that empaths sense the vibrations and "feel" of the human aura. The aura is the naturally occurring energy field that surrounds all living things. It can be seen, felt, and even photographed. Every aura is unique, and it leaves traces behind, no matter where you go. The aura may, in fact, linger around objects or places and that "lingering energy" is what an empath senses and intuits. I should also point out here that the ability to read objects is called psychometry.

In psychometry, an empath senses a person's energy that lingers on an object, such as a ring, for example. They read this information through touch and can deduce information about the individual's personality and life, whether they are living or deceased. They sense and feel on an emotional level who the person truly is (or was). This psychometric ability is strongly tied into the emotions, just as you'd expect with an empath.

The psychic reception area for an empath is located in the solar plexus region and is linked to the same chakra point. In this area of the body there are tons of nerve networks, and they flare out over the abdomen like an intricate web. This chakra point is tied into your creativity and your emotions, which takes the mystery right out of why this is an empath's power center. With an empath, it's all about how they feel: what emotions they pick up and what sentiments they sense.

Empaths can be overly sensitive to touch from a stranger or may dislike crowds, antiques, or environments such as hospitals. So they have to learn how to "toughen up" and block overwhelming memories and sensations. I'm not being unsympathetic here; I'm one of those people who is very empathic. It can be tough, but I learned how to block and shield so I wouldn't be so overwhelmed by other people, their memories, and emotions all the time.

For empaths, psychic protection is a necessity. Take the time to ground yourself and to "zip up" those chakras so you don't become bombarded with other people's negativity and bad vibes. Visualize a shield of blue light surrounding you. Also, I have found that folding your arms across your middle will block out any negative emotions as well. This gesture physically blocks all those psychic receptors in the solar plexus region, and it muffles them, giving you an immediate break.

Also, in a pinch, if you are feeling bombarded with other people's emotions, try washing your hands—running cold water over your hands will break the emotional link. Just quietly excuse yourself to go to the restroom. This gives you the opportunity to walk away from an overwhelming situation or person that you are picking up on. Once you have physically removed yourself from the situation or person, ground yourself and then follow that up by washing your hands. Quick, clever, and very, very effective.

In magick, empaths have a built-in safety net to keep them from even considering negative work. Why? Because it's very easy for an empath to understand exactly how it would feel to be on the receiving end of manipulative magick. On the plus side, empathy can help you work a spell for another. Your emotions are easily matched to theirs, and this can be a large help while working, let's say, a requested healing spell for another person. With empaths, their emotions and compassion always lead their magick. So if this is your strongest trait, then celebrate it, and let your sentiments guide you into strong, beautiful, compassionate, and ethical magick.

For whereas the mind works in possibilities,

the intuitions work in actualities, and when

you intuitively desire, that is possible to you.

Whereas what you mentally or "consciously" desire

is nine times out of ten impossible; hitch your wagon

to a star, or you will just stay where you are.

D. H. LAWRENCE

EMBRACING YOUR INTUITION

Now that you have this information, you can get a better understanding of your own unique psychic gifts. It will help you to understand your abilities and talents if you validate and document them as you go along. If you ignore your intuition and your psychic abilities, they will sulk or won't "speak" to you at all, making it much harder for you to coax them back out. Get a little notebook and jot down your psychic experiences, and then follow them up with a quick note so you can keep track of how things turned out. Validating the experiences is key; it also helps you figure things out.

For example, for years I would have soft, fuzzy dreams of a baby girl who would crawl through a room where I was sitting. She would babble at me, smile, and then crawl away. I would leap up to chase after her while she giggled at me and crawled even faster. As soon as I'd get close enough to scoop her up, I would wake up from the dream.

When my kids were small, that dream scared me to death. I wrongly assumed, at first, that it meant I was pregnant again (three kids were plenty for my husband and me).

Then, after a while, I realized that every time I had this dream, it was simply a way of telling me it was about someone else—that another baby was on its way to a close friend or family member—which took the stress right out of the experience, let me tell you!

At last count, we are up to sixteen nieces and nephews. So over the years she has shown up a lot in my dreams, whether the baby is a boy or girl. Now I know whenever I have this dream that within a week we usually receive some happy news.

Only once has this dream changed on me. That one time in the dream, as I went to scoop her up, instead of waking up I found the baby sitting in front of me, spelling out the name "Elizabeth" in alphabet blocks. Then I woke up, surprised and startled at the new twist on my familiar dream. I stayed quiet about that new information, wrote it down in my dream journal, and waited. Sure enough, a new nephew and then a niece arrived within a year—and my niece's parents announced, after she was born, that her middle name would be Elizabeth.

Remember, for the most part, that psychic impressions are quiet and subtle. So don't worry about them. The only time they are loud or full blast is if the message is vitally important or you are in danger. If for some reason you experience this, then pay attention, and be smart and safe. Think of those psychic warnings like signposts on a road. Pay attention and make the appropriate detours, if necessary. Forewarned is forearmed. Be aware and pay attention. Work the exercises that were listed earlier in this chapter, and have fun! Use the journal pages in this book to start a dream journal, and see what you learn. Figure out where your talents lie, and then add this knowledge to the magick you already practice.

In our next chapter, we will discover the psychic tides and energies of the moon. This will provide you with even more opportunities to crank up the volume on your own individual style of magick. Just imagine all of the new ways you'll be able to think about your Witchcraft and natural magick! Once you start down this intuitive path, it will quite naturally lead you straight to your own inner wisdom. Go ahead, embrace your psychic abilities—and let's add another wonderful dimension to your natural witchery.

Chapter 2

Soon as the evening shades prevail,

The moon takes up the wondrous tale,

And nightly to the listening earth

Repeats the story of her birth . . .

JOSEPH ADDISON

The Psychic Cycles of the Moon

No other natural object has been more venerated throughout time than our closest companion in the sky, the moon. Moon mythology stretches far back into our history, and every country and culture has its own legends and tales about lunar deities. For Witches, the ever-changing moon symbolizes the Triple Goddess in her aspects of Maiden, Mother, and Crone. Our mystical and mysterious moon has a feminine power that is associated with intuition, magick, and psychic themes.

In ancient times, the moon was important to the people for a number of reasons. First and most obviously, it was a source of light in the night sky. The moon was also a time keeper, as the ancient people counted the moon's cycles, making the first calendar of sorts. The moon also regulated the ocean's tides and the migratory movement of the earth's creatures.

All people are affected by the moon—women in particular, due to the obvious connections between the moon's phases and their menstrual cycles and fertility. Men also are influenced by the moon, but they need to pay attention to these subtle changes. In years past, this was a much more basic and "earthy" connection, as the moon was utilized in the ancient peoples' calculations and plans as hunters and gatherers. The men carefully watched the full moons come and go, noting the seasonal changes and the movement of the animals. The knowledge of the most opportune time to plant and to harvest crops, as well as the most favorable time to fish and hunt, was an integral part of their mysteries.

Learning how to work with the intuitive energies of the moon today helps us to attune with the rhythm of natural energy within our own lives. In truth, all the cycles of the moon generate their own type of psychic energy and magick, for lunar energies are both feminine and receptive. Make no mistake, whether you are male or female, they do influence your moods, psychic abilities, magick, and your life. This is important to realize, since psychic powers are receptive in nature—and by that I mean you receive the images and impressions. When you work in accord with these lunar tides, you draw in Goddess energy. This lunar power attracts and pulls in; receptive energy is magnetic, as it draws whatever it desires to itself.

The Goddess and the power of the moon are popular topics of discussion among Witches, Pagans, and magick users. However, many folks sort of miss the forest for the trees when it comes to the Goddess, magick, and the moon. So, before you roll your eyes and let out an aggrieved sigh, thinking that I'm going to launch into a basic Wicca 101 topic that you already know ... hold on for a second. There is further information to be gained on this subject other than just the typical correspondences of "Maiden: waxing moon; Mother: full moon; and Crone: waning moon." When was the last time you *really* paid attention to how the phases of the moon affected both your intuition and your psychic sensitivity?

As the moon is a natural representation for the Goddess, you may want to pause and reconsider all the various moon phases and the psychic energies that they bring into your spellcasting. Both the Goddess and the moon are ever-changing. They have many aspects or faces and myriad lessons to reveal. I suggest you take a walk outside at night and spend some time under the moon's transforming light. Open up your heart and expand your psychic abilities. Allow your intuition to lead you, and the illumination of the Goddess will shine down on you.

Lady Moon, Lady Moon, where are you roving?

A Children's Song

Drawing Down the Moon

The act of drawing down the moon is a powerful psychic and magickal experience. By focusing on the light of the full moon, you are actually drawing the Goddess into your own body. Again, realize that lunar energy is intuitive, magnetic, and receptive. This is a force of nature, and tapping into this power is a transformative experience. This type of empowerment needs to be felt, and it's going to be different for each individual.

I have heard this process explained and intellectualized to death, but the truth is this is a silent ritual. It requires no tools or props other than yourself and the full moon. Learning to draw down the moon is an intuitive and personal experience that marks a significant step of your journey. This is an important part of natural witchery, for now you are beginning to make your magick both intuitive and personal.

No words are needed while you draw down the moon. If you'd like to say a few words in greeting before you get started, go right ahead. Typically I look up, smile at the moon, and say, "Hello, Goddess." Seems to me that a simple and heartfelt greeting is much more eloquent than fumbling around trying desperately to remember that lengthy, dramatic poem you memorized. The Goddess does not require melodrama. Just be yourself, and follow your own insights. The following steps for the process are straightforward ones, and as we've seen, simple is usually the best.

- Step outside and stand under the light of the full moon. Too basic for you? Hmm, you'd be surprised. You have to get outside for this one, folks.

- Ground and center yourself. Imagine that your feet are like the roots of a tree, and sink them down into the earth. Visualize that any stress or anger you may be carrying is draining away to be absorbed back harmlessly into the earth. Now see that the earth is in turn sending you revitalizing energy. Raise up your arms, and stretch out your fingers. Take a nice deep cleansing breath and blow it out slowly.

- Next, you may stand with your hands loosely at your sides, holding your hands palms up. I have seen people dramatically throw their arms out wide and embrace the night sky. Go with whatever position feels more natural to you. If you are concerned that someone (like a curious neighbor) may be watching, then just keep your arms down and stand in a relaxed pose.

- Now open up your chakras. Just as we practiced in the previous chapter, light up those seven energy centers, stretch out your psychic feelings, and open yourself up to the Goddess and her illumination.

- Tip up your face to the light of the moon, and envision pulling some of that luminosity and power down and inside of yourself. Give yourself a few moments, and feel the difference that it makes. For example, if you feel down and self-conscious, you will likely stand taller and be more confident after drawing down the moon. If you feel overwhelmed and stressed out, you'll notice that your shoulders will relax, and you will feel more at peace when you are finished. You may feel a shivery and tingling connection with other Witches from all over the world. Or you may feel a comforting warmth surrounding you, like an astral hug, telling you that She is looking down on you and smiling. Enjoy the sensations for a while.

- Take a deep breath, and let it out slowly. Now zip your chakras closed with a quick arm motion from your mid-thigh area to over the top of your head. Ground and center again. Relax.

- Whisper a "thank you" to the Goddess. Return indoors.

- If you'd like, take notes and write down in your journal or Book of Shadows what you experienced. (Also, I'll let you in on a little secret: the various full moons throughout the year do carry different energies. The harvest moon feels electric and mysterious, while a winter full moon seems wise and silent; a summer full moon has a lazy, mellow quality as compared to the energy and excitement of a spring full moon. Keep track and note what differences you personally experience.)

Okay, so how'd you do? Everyone will experience this gift from the Goddess in their own way. Do not, I repeat, *do not* think this process to death. Just get out there and experience it. Before we close up this section, here is a little more food for thought. Traditionally, drawing down the moon is performed at the full moon phase. However, try working this exercise at several different lunar phases, like the new crescent just after sunset or the waning moon in the early morning hours, and see what sort of results you achieve then.

Want more information on the other mystical lunar phases? Well, in our next section we will examine the various phases of the moon and what magick and psychic abilities are affected by them. Oh, and there are a few lunar spells in there for you to work as well.

> *Late yester evening I saw the new moon,*
> *With the old moon in her arm.*
> THOMAS PERCY

THE PSYCHIC AND MAGICKAL MOON PHASES

There is a subtle and enchanting rhythm to the mood of each month and the lunar cycles as they roll from one into the other. By working in harmony with these lunar tides, you can easily turn up the volume on your magick, especially when you recognize and work in accord with your intuition and personal psychic abilities.

Now that you have acknowledged your psychic talents, you can embrace the ability to be receptive. For receptive power is not passive, it is magnetic, compelling, and captivating. This type of energy draws intuition, magick, and power straight to you. Receptive lunar power will also boost your inspiration and facilitate the effectiveness of your magick.

How, you may wonder? Because the power of the lunar phases profoundly influences all life on the planet as well as human behavior. Working with and acknowledging the cycles of the moon allows us to arrange our magick in the most opportune way. Just as certain types of magick will coordinate with either the waxing or waning moon, so too will your psychic abilities be affected by the ever-changing lunar tides and energies. The trick here, my friends, is to learn to work with these psychic energies in harmony with nature and your magick.

Listed below are four major lunar phases and the accompanying psychic and magickal information. There is a coordinating psychic spell listed, and the deity aspects of the Maiden, Mother, and Crone are listed as well. May this information shed a little moonlight on the subject for you.

First Quarter

(From the new moon to the waxing half moon.) As the slim crescent moon slowly becomes fuller each night, now is the time to begin new projects, to be creative, to meet new people, and to be outgoing. Your personal psychic energy will be building, and you will notice you are more sympathetic and sensitive to other people's positive emotions at this time. Awaken your intuition and pay attention, for as the moon grows brighter your dreams and their meanings will become clearer. Here is the ideal time for magick and spells that draw things to you. Pull that affirmative change and bubbling energy straight into your life and reap the benefits. The waxing moon is a time to celebrate growth and potential. As the moon grows larger, your magickal goals will manifest. This moon phase corresponds with the Maiden aspect of the Goddess, such as Athena, Artemis/Diana, and Bast.

Second Quarter

(From the waxing half moon to the full moon.) During this lunar phase, emotions and instinct are heightened. You will notice that precognitive dreams, intuition, and clairvoyance will peak as the full moon gets closer. During this lunar phase, spells will come to fruition swiftly, especially if they are uncomplicated and sincere. The closer you can cast your spells to the actual time of the full moon, the more power and *oomph* your spells and charms will have. Now, the day of the full moon is actually a time of maximum magickal power. This is an all-purpose lunar phase, so get in there and start casting! The full moon aligns with the Mother aspect of the Goddess; for example, Selene, Luna, Freya, Isis, or Aphrodite.

Third Quarter

(From the second night after the full moon to the waning half moon.) When the moon begins to wane, its light slowly dissipates in the night sky. This is a powerful time of internal energy and an opportunity to quietly look within. Focus on dreams, instincts, and gut hunches. If you are clairaudient, pay particular attention to those internal messages. While the moon wanes, work magick to remove negativity and obstacles that you are facing. During this lunar phase, work magick to carefully dissolve problems, push away troubles, and remove negativity in the best way possible for all those concerned. As the moon wanes, so too will the situation or problem. The third-quarter moon corresponds to the Crone aspect of the Goddess, such as Cerridwen, Hecate, or Nepthys.

Fourth Quarter

(From the waning half moon until the dark of the moon.) This is the dark time of the moon. You may find that your psychic talents take a little vacation during the dark phases of the moon, or, on the other hand, they may come roaring to life with an all-out bombardment on your senses. Personally, I have found that abilities such as empathy and psychometry are more pronounced at this time. Why, you may wonder? Well, I have found that this type of psychic ability forces you to look within and to be still as the information comes to you—what better time than in the waning moon, when your powers are focused internally? Magickally, now is the occasion to tackle serious issues, such as extreme protection magick, bindings, or banishings, and keeping away criminals, prowlers, or stalkers. Casting your spells in the final days of the moon's cycle (when the moon is not visible at all) will increase the force behind your banishing and protective magick. This phase of the moon is often linked to the darker aspects of the Goddess, when she is a spiritual warrior; again, Hecate is a good one to work with in this phase, but you can also call on Sekhmet, the Morrigan, or even Kali, if you are really feeling brave.

PSYCHIC SPELLS FOR THE FOUR MOON PHASES

Supplies

- A white tealight candle
- A clear candleholder cup
- A small magnet (to represent the moon's magnetism and "pull" in your life)
- A lighter or matches
- A safe, flat surface to set up on

Directions

Set the candle inside the candleholder, and place the magnet in front of it. If you choose, you can jazz up these spells with silver glitter sprinkled on your work surface. Or how about a silver or white altar cloth, or fresh white flowers tucked in a vase? Try fragrant flowers such as white roses, lilies, freesia, or daisies.

Once you have things arranged to your liking, take a moment to ground and center. Visualize all the fresh energies that the moon in her various phases provides. When you are ready, light the candle and repeat the spell corresponding to the moon phase you are in three times. Allow the candle to burn out in a safe place when you are finished. Please note: tealights take about four hours to burn.

First Quarter Moon Spell

This lunar spell encourages fresh starts and helps you to sense the magnetic and feminine powers of the moon. At this time, your psychic abilities will begin to burgeon out and your empathy will increase.

Increase my sensitivity during this first lunar phase

Bringing fresh starts and inspired magick into all my days

Lunar powers are magnetic, they do pull in positive change

May the Maiden goddess hear my call and bless me in many ways.

Second Quarter Moon Spell

This lunar spell calls for you to ride the psychic wave with the increasing lunar energies and light of the moon as it grows fuller each night. This is a good "opening spell" to use in a ritual throughout this waxing lunar phase.

As the moon rolls through its second phase, magick will surely grow.

The gifts of sight, dreams, and intuition now begin to flow.

Bless my spells with extra power, may I use my gifts wisely,

While the Mother's moon waxes full, shining love straight down on me.

Third Quarter Moon Spell

The following lunar spell works in harmony with the waning moon. This is the point in time where you work magick to remove obstacles and problems. This is the time of the clairaudient's greatest powers, so focus those psychic abilities internally and listen carefully for messages and wisdom. The magick is inside you. Be still, and let it unfold.

As the moon starts to wane, the third lunar cycle begins,

So look quietly within, reflect, and soul-search again.

Work to remove problems now, spells I'll carefully weave,

As the moon grows smaller, so too will my troubles leave.

Fourth Quarter Moon Spell

Finally, here is a spell for the final phase of the moon. This is the Crone's moon, and at this time your psychic gifts may be at their strongest. As the energy turns to a hushed, waiting mode, it doesn't mean it's gone, just that it is extremely focused and internal. So if you aren't paying attention, you may not pick up on those psychic impressions. If this is a problem for you, ask the wise old Crone for her assistance. As far as magick is concerned, this is the time to deal with those more serious issues. Check out the final line of this spell and adjust as necessary for your purposes; for example, the word "protection" can be easily switched to "banishing."

The Crone's moon grows smaller at the passing of each eve.

For this magick to work, in myself I must believe.

Charms performed now require a wisdom most sublime

The protection spell is now cast, sealed up with a rhyme.

That orbed maiden with white fire laden

whom mortals call the moon.

PERCY BYSSHE SHELLEY

ENCHANTING LUNAR ECLIPSES

If there is ever an opportunity to cash in on a phenomenal period of natural psychic and magickal power, it is during a lunar eclipse. These celestial events offer us a wonderful chance to work very powerful intuitive magick. Over the years, I have noticed that on the day of a lunar eclipse my psychic abilities get turned up to full volume. And I have also discovered that any type of moon magick is especially potent if performed during the lunar eclipse.

Why? Well, during the eclipse, the moon appears to go through all of its phases in a few hours—so you can literally tap into each phase of the moon in a brief period of time. As you watch the moon roll through that lunar eclipse, you are experiencing one of nature's most incredible shows. It is easy to imagine how in ancient times an eclipse filled people with awe. Seeing the moon change in front of your very eyes surely had to be the work of the gods. Actually, a friend of mine once described the lunar eclipse to her young daughters as a time when the Goddess slowly pulls her burgundy cape across the moon, which I think is a wonderful visualization.

Technically, an eclipse occurs when one celestial object passes into the shadow cast by another—as with an eclipse of the moon, when the moon falls under Earth's shadow. If this occurs during a full moon, where the moon will travel through Earth's shadow, it is called a lunar eclipse.

Much to my surprise, the term *solar eclipse* is a misnomer; an *occultation* is the correct term for a solar eclipse. The term *occult*, in fact, means "hidden." And according to astronomical terminology, an occultation is defined as an event that occurs when one heavenly body passes in front of and hides or blocks another. For example, in a classic solar eclipse, the moon is at its new phase, and it passes in front of and blocks, or "occults," the sun—as seen from Earth. The moon casts a shadow on Earth, and, depending on the viewer's location, if they are under the path of the shadow, they see the event as a total solar eclipse.

Okay, so you probably remember your earth science classes from middle school, and you are all set to tell me how you already understand the mechanics of an eclipse. But as I researched this lunar section of the book, a few lunar terms kept popping up, and after consideration I decided that they are important words to add to any Witch's vocabulary—especially as you are studying lunar magick. For example, do you know what *earthshine* is? I had noticed this during waxing and waning crescent moons for years, but I never knew it had a technical term.

Also, did you know there are four different types of lunar eclipses? Ever wonder what they are? Well, you'll find them right here in the following list of terms. Read over these terms and add some new information to your magickal studies. I've yet to meet a Witch or magickal practitioner who wasn't always on the lookout for something new to learn!

Terms & Types of Lunar Eclipses

APOGEE—When the moon is at its farthest point from Earth: 252,700 miles away.

BLUE MOON—The second full moon that occurs within one calendar month.

EARTHSHINE—The dark, smoky portion of the moon that you can see shining alongside a brilliant crescent. Described as seeing "the old moon within the new moon's arms."

HARVEST MOON—The full moon closest to the Autumn Equinox. Typically these occur in September; however, one out of three harvest moons do fall in the month of October.

LUNATION—One lunar cycle phase.

OCCULTATION—An astronomical event that happens when one celestial body passes in front of another, making an object partially or fully hidden in the sky, such as a solar "eclipse."

PARTIAL LUNAR ECLIPSE—When only part of the moon enters the umbra (the umbra being the darker inner section of Earth's shadow).

PENUMBRA—The outer part of Earth's shadow where sunlight is not completely blocked during an eclipse. It only dims the moon slightly.

PENUMBRAL LUNAR ECLIPSE—This occurs when the moon only passes through Earth's outer section of the shadow, the penumbra.

PERIGEE—When the moon is the closest distance to Earth, at 221,550 miles. If the perigee falls on a full moon phase, the moon will look slightly larger than normal.

TOTAL LUNAR ECLIPSE—This occurs when the moon goes entirely into Earth's darkest, most inner part of the shadow, the umbra.

TOTAL PENUMBRAL ECLIPSE—A rare type of lunar eclipse where the eclipse stays only within the penumbra section of Earth's shadow, but the sections of the moon closest to the umbra will look a bit darker than the rest of the moon.

TOTALITY—The phase of an eclipse when it is total.

UMBRA—This is the region of the complete, darkest shadow created by Earth in an eclipse. In lunar eclipses it has a reddish hue.

ZENITH—The point in the sky directly above the viewer. Also the highest point of the moon's—or the sun's—arc across the sky.

With hue like that when some great painter dips

His pencil in the gloom of earthquake and eclipse.

PERCY BYSSHE SHELLEY

THE COLORS AND MAGICKS
OF A LUNAR ECLIPSE

While the moon doesn't completely disappear during a lunar eclipse, it does change color—sometimes dramatically. As the moon passes through the umbra, the color effect will depend on the amount of refracted light and the number of clouds in the atmosphere blocking that light. This causes the moon to have a reddish hue that can vary widely from one eclipse to another. And there is a way to rate the color of a lunar eclipse.

This scale was devised by a celebrated French astronomer named André-Louis Danjon (1890–1967). He recorded the brightness measurements using this method, which came to be called the "Danjon Scale," for over twenty-five years. In 1958, he was awarded the Gold Medal of the Royal Astronomical Society. Here is the color rating scale:

0   Very dark eclipse: The moon looks almost invisible

1   Dark eclipse: grey or brownish color, difficult to see

2   Deep red, burgundy, or rust-colored eclipse, with a very dark central part in the umbra and the outer rim of the umbra relatively bright

3   Brick-red eclipse, typically with a bright or yellow rim to the umbra

4   Very bright copper or orange-colored eclipse, with a bluish, very bright umbral rim

MAGICKAL CORRESPONDENCES FOR THE COLORS OF A LUNAR ECLIPSE

I thought it would be interesting to add the traditional color magick correspondences to this color scale to see what I came up with, and the results were fascinating, to say the least. Keep in mind that it's going to be tough to predict the color of the lunar eclipse. You are going to have to live on the edge and be spontaneous once you see what sort of color you are going to experience. I suggest waiting until the eclipse hits its peak or totality, then you can go from there.

0   During a deep and dark-toned lunar eclipse, work spells and charms for protections, banishings, and bindings.

1   For this rating, with that dark grey or brown color, try working glamouries or spells for neutrality or invisibility, or to make your actions go unnoticed.

2   The dark red hue corresponds with the Mother aspect of the Goddess, as well as healing, love, and protection magick.

3   An eclipse that rates a 3 on the scale, with a red moon and bright yellow rim, may be a perfect complement to transformation spells or magick that increases your psychic knowledge and reception.

4   Finally, an orange-looking eclipse could be worked for magick that increases your personal power and for success.

Also, don't forget to experiment with this color list and see what you come up with. Use your intuition and work with the color associations of your own tradition. The most powerful magick is individual and custom-made to suit your needs.

LUNAR ECLIPSE RITUAL TO
INCREASE PSYCHIC TALENTS

On average, there are two lunar eclipses during the year, so you will have a few chances during the year to experiment with this ritual. How do you find out exactly when and in what location viewing will be the best? Hit the Internet. Some of the better sites I have found for eclipse information are listed in this book's bibliography. While this spell is to increase your psychic abilities, you have other options for magick during a lunar eclipse as well. Eclipse magick may also be utilized for transformation, protection, prosperity, or healing, but don't stop there. Use your imagination and decide for yourself. Personally, I like to save eclipse magick for important or "big guns" type of work. And personal transformation seems to fall into that category, as far as I'm concerned.

Note: As the lunar eclipse will take a few hours to work its way through its cycle, keep in mind that this ritual will take a few hours of your time. Plan ahead and make yourself comfortable during this ritual. Remember the ritual will last as long as the eclipse does, so you're going to be there a while.

Consider dragging a sleeping bag to the backyard or sitting in a lawn chair on your porch—whatever works. In a pinch, during a very cold winter eclipse I once stayed inside and lay across my bed watching the moon change through the bedroom windows. My children were very young at the time, so I let them stay up for a while and watch the eclipse with me. Yup, you guessed it, the Witch and her young brood all attired in their flannel pajamas. It was very cosmopolitan and chic. Once the kids all dropped off to sleep, I bundled them back to bed and then took notes on my experiences during the rest of the event and meditated.

To work the following lunar eclipse ritual, set up your supplies an hour or so ahead of the event, and then while the moon is covered with that dusky-looking shadow, you can work the following ritual for personal transformation and to increase your psychic abilities. You will notice a difference in your perception levels during this ritual, so be prepared to note your experiences in your journal. (Oh—and flannel PJs are strictly optional!)

Supplies

- One white taper candle (for the full moon)
- One burgundy taper candle (to represent the shadow falling across the moon)
- Two candlestick holders
- Matches or a lighter
- A safe, flat surface to set up on
- Your Book of Shadows or journal to take notes in
- Pencil or pen

Directions

Light the two tapers—first the white, then the burgundy. Sit and meditate for a moment or two on the changes you'd like to bring about. Repeat the following charm just as the eclipse begins. Then once the spell is spoken, go and find yourself a good, comfortable spot to watch one of nature's finest shows.

> *As the Goddess pulls her soft cloak across the face of the moon,*
> *I light a dark and white candle to bring transformation soon.*

As the eclipse shows all the lunar phases so bright,

May my psychic talents be seen in a whole new light.

As the eclipse finishes, close up your spell with this line:

By the powers of the moon, earth, and sun,

So mote it be, and let it harm none.

Allow the eclipse spell candles to burn in a safe place until they go out on their own.

Let the air strike our tune,

Whilst we show reverence to yond peeping moon.

THOMAS MIDDLETON

BEWITCHING BLUE MOONS

In modern folklore, a blue moon is defined as the second full moon to fall within one calendar month. Why is it called a blue moon, you may wonder? This popular title started in the early 1900s and appears to have originated from the phrase "once in a blue moon"—meaning the event was rare. So has the moon ever actually appeared blue? Yes, after a major volcanic eruption. When the volcanic ash rose up into the atmosphere, the ash clouds made the moon appear a blueish color.

Blue moons occur once every thirty-two to thirty-three months, on average. And in 1999 there were double blue moons. Since that year's February had only 28 days and the lunar cycles were favorable, both January and March had two full moons each. If you missed out on this event, you can catch the double blue moons again; they happen approximately every nineteen solar years. Look for double blue moons to make their appearance in the year 2018 and in 2037; again, these events will occur in January and March.

For Witches today, the blue moon is a time of incredible magick and mystery. On the night of a blue moon, the magickal energy is powerful and extremely long-lasting, as spells cast on the night of a blue moon are said to hold until the *next* blue moon.

How's that for an enduring spell? I can just imagine you rubbing your hands together and gleefully plotting! The night of a blue moon is a fantastic time to work for love, protection, wisdom, or to try your hand at divination. A classic lunar goddess to work with is Selene. This Greco-Roman full moon goddess is one of my favorite deities. Selene is especially generous to Witches and is known and well loved for her speedy and practical magickal solutions. One of my favorite lunar spells I wrote years ago is to increase intuition and to gain the wisdom to use this new information intelligently. It works out beautifully when you call on Selene and combine it with the energies of a blue moon. Try it out for yourself.

A Blue Moon Spell for Wisdom and Intuition

Supplies

- One blue candle (your choice as to the size or style: taper or votive)
- One white candle (again, your choice as to the style and size)
- Two coordinating candleholders
- A small representation of each of the four elements; try a crystal for earth, a seashell for water, a feather for air, a lava rock for fire (or the flames from the spell candles will work nicely too)
- A fresh white flower in a bud vase (for Selene—try a white rose, lily, or carnation, or try bluebells, which are one of Selene's favorites)
- A lighter or matches
- A safe, flat surface to set up on

Directions

Arrange the items as you prefer. Light the blue candle to represent the blue moon and then the white candle for the moon goddess Selene. Make sure to keep the flower back from the candle flames. Ground and center yourself, and then draw down the moon. Afterwards, tip up your face to the light of the blue moon and make your request for wisdom and protection:

> *On this night of Selene's magickal blue moon,*
> *Lady, hear my request and grant me a boon.*
> *Bless me with intuition and wisdom both day and night.*
> *Work your loving magick in each aspect of my life.*

Close up the spell with:

> *I thank the goddess Selene for her time and care,*
>
> *As this blue moon gently hovers in the night air.*

Ground and center yourself again. Allow the candles to burn until they go out on their own. Tidy up your workspace when the candles are finished. Keep the flower in the vase someplace where you will enjoy it—until it begins to fade, then dispose of the flower neatly by giving it back to nature. Add it to a compost pile or bury it in your garden.

> *May you have warm words on a cold evening,*
>
> *A full moon on a dark night,*
>
> *And the road downhill all the way to your door.*
>
> FAMILIAR SAYING

THAT MAGICKAL MOON

I hope that you will enjoy experimenting with and trying out all of this chapter's various spells, charms, and rituals. Get out there under the nighttime sky and discover all of the lunar phases. Work magick under a blue moon and during a dramatic lunar eclipse. Keep in mind that the moon is an icon for magick, the divine feminine, and our intuition. I expect that you have learned a few new tricks and been reinspired to work magick with the psychic tides and enchanting energies of the moon. It's a perfect way to revitalize your witchery.

The psychic energy of the moon still holds sway over us, and it is an undeniable magickal force in our lives. The ever-changing moon is both a companion and a guide. Its radiance brings an incredible amount of illumination to our magickal journey. So tip up your face to its silver light and walk with confidence and wisdom while traveling along your own spiritual path.

Chapter 3

Knowledge is power.

FRANCIS BACON

Personal Power

Now that your intuition is up and humming, we can turn our focus to personal power, the next step in natural witchery. Here is where we begin to make the magick more individual. I mean, honestly, don't you want your magick to have some character? Just a little something special that separates you from everyone else? Of course you do. By discovering your personal power, you'll crank up the level of your expertise and put the focus on your own individual style of magick.

We are going to accomplish this by taking a deeper look into the elements of earth, air, fire, and water, and how they play out and affect our magickal selves. Our personalities are a wonderful mixture of the qualities of the four elements. And while it is certainly true that we each feel an affinity to a certain natural element or elements from time to time, we need to be in balance to harmoniously employ all four. It is important to reflect on each of the elements and to consider how you individually experience magick through all four of them. Then allow those elements to flow into your life.

To boost your personal power and to have it up and running at top speed, you will need to get—well, for lack of a better word—"personal," and do a little soul-searching.

After all, the best individual to transform your life and help you reclaim your own powers is, of course, you.

The power of the elements and all of nature is deep and infinite, and the following elemental information is not a 101 rehash. Truthfully, this type of knowledge is vital for everyone; this includes the more experienced or advanced practitioners too. For years I always thought that to be an "advanced Witch" meant you had somehow discovered all these phenomenal mysteries of the cosmos—when in actuality what you begin to discover is that those basic lessons you first learned have many hidden layers. The longer you study and practice, the more of those levels you will begin to explore and uncover. There truly are worlds within worlds.

Study and take the time to search inside yourself and to uncover the hidden, layered powers of the natural elements. These lessons will be a bit different for everyone. That's what makes this type of magick so special, because you are adding dimension to your craft.

By using your intuition—and stretching out those psychic abilities that we worked on in the first section of this book—you will begin to see how each of the four natural elements play out within your magickal personality. Why is this so darn important, anyway? Because you will gain an understanding of your elemental strengths and your weaknesses. For your magickal power to be its most effective, you have to take a little private inventory and then remove any imbalances or blocks. This in turn allows you to focus and fine-tune your magick, and turn up the level of your personal power. To begin our lesson of self-discovery, look over the following elemental personality traits and see which ones you most closely identify with.

ELEMENTAL PERSONALITIES

I say the whole earth and all the stars in the sky

are for religion's sake.

WALT WHITMAN

Earth

Our first element, earth, is associated with the planet, fields of ripe grain, the forest, woodlands, and the garden; it also corresponds to the Witch's Pyramid adage "to be silent." Earth magick is a feminine energy (think of Gaia, the earth mother), and its power can be accessed through herbs, plants, flowers, and crystals. To be an earth person is to be practical, realistic, and tactile. These grounded folks who are "down to earth" care about what is real, physical, and what they can do and experience for themselves. Earth people are methodical and patient as they work toward their goals. Tactile people, they enjoy working with their hands and may be into various arts and crafts like floral design, woodworking, painting, and knitting. They like to be able to touch what they create, and texture and beauty are important to them.

Earth people are homebodies and create beautiful, welcoming homes. They are marriage-minded and go for long-lasting, solid relationships. They are physical and unabashedly enjoy their sexuality and love to laugh. Earth people are the touchers of the world—a pat on the back, a welcoming hug. Negative earth qualities may result in their being called a "stick in the mud." Other less-attractive traits include being very resistant to change, stubbornness, and being bullheaded.

Physically, earth people need to be careful, as they tend to have round body shapes. It's not that they are lazy, it's that there is a lot of fire energy in hard exercise—so an earth person would rather not exercise. An earth person's idea of exercise includes a nice leisurely stroll through the park or tending to their yards and gardens.

> I breathed a song into the air,
>
> It fell to earth, I knew not where.
>
> HENRY WADSWORTH LONGFELLOW

Air

The air is associated with the sky, wind, clouds, mountaintops, and birds of all sorts. This element corresponds with the Witch's Pyramid adage "to know." Air symbolizes freedom and spaciousness. It is light, expansive, and damn near impossible to truly measure or contain. Air is ever expanding, like breath. Ideas are said to come from the element of air, as does inspiration—a word that means "to breath in." The element of air is one of intellect. It reflects the metaphysical principle of life. Air is associated with new life and beginnings—anything that "dawns," whether that's the day that dawns or a thought that suddenly dawns on you. Through the magick of the element of air, you receive the inspiration for deciding which direction in life you wish to take.

People who have a lot of air qualities in their personality will think before they feel; they are rational and intelligent. Some folks who have strong links to this element can be the academic type. They are also fluently clever, witty, and express themselves clearly, whether it's through speaking or writing. Air is the element of communication, so these folks may be fabulous lecturers, entertaining teachers, and sharp and witty conversationalists. Air people like to have several things going at one time; they are the ultimate multitaskers.

However, too much air energy can make them seem like they are absent-minded, or that they appear to have their heads in the clouds or are airheads. Air people may be brilliant but out of step with the world around them. They may be incredibly smart but not be able to remember or complete the most mundane of tasks. These over-airy individuals may spend too much time in their own heads and simply ignore the physical world around them.

> *The fire upon the hearth is low,*
> *And there is stillness everywhere,*
> *And, like winged spirits, here and there*
> *The firelight shadows fluttering go.*
> EUGENE FIELD

Fire

Fire is associated with the sun, volcanoes, wildfires, deserts, tropical climates, and rock gardens. This blazing element corresponds with the Witch's Pyramid adage "to dare." Traditionally, fire is the element of illumination and transformation. It is associated with the divine spark or the spark of the soul. Fire magick can be accessed through candle, color, and solar spells. People who have a lot of fire qualities in their personality will be warm, passionate, and courageous. Fire is sometimes linked to intuition, and it's definitely part of taking the initiative to bring about positive change.

Fire represents both the light of intelligence and the flash of courage that allows you to follow through with your dreams and ideas. Sunlight is also within the realm of the element of fire. The strength and power of the sun should not be overlooked in this element. After all, the sun does bring light and illumination to our days, does it not?

Individuals with plenty of fiery energy are often strongly intuitive. They believe in and fight for a worthy cause. Fire folks are natural leaders, the movers and shakers. Someone who has lots of fire energy will compel others to pay attention to them. Fire people are fascinating and sexual. These individuals make impassioned lovers and may be flamboyant and romantic.

If someone carries too much fire energy, they can be impulsive, quick-tempered, display violent tempers, or be prone to rage. They may also be the type who silently hold a grudge and carry around anger for a long time. They simmer, stew, and occasionally boil over. To carry too much fire energy is to run the risk of becoming obsessive.

Smooth runs the water where the brook is deep.

SHAKESPEARE

Water

Water is associated with streams, rivers, springs, oceans, lakes, and life-giving rain. This element corresponds with the Witch's Pyramid adage "to will." Just to keep things interesting, the moon is closely linked to the element of water, as the moon affects the tides of the oceans and all life on the planet. Water is in all life. It brings freshness and fullness. Water is also the element of dreams, the subconscious, trance, vision, and clairvoyance. Psychic abilities and loving emotions are said to come from the element of water and from the moon. Emotions are naturally linked to this element, as they are often described as "welling up" or "springing forth."

Water people are sensitive souls. They are the natural empaths, and their emotions rule them. Also, other people's feelings are of utmost importance to a water personality. Water people have open, romantic hearts and are generous, sympathetic, and empathic. They are the mystics, the romantic lovers, and the dreamers. They may become artists, therapists, healers, mystics, and musicians. These individuals have a sensuous grace; they are elegant and prefer flowing, soft clothes.

Folks who carry too much water energy are brooders, moody and deep. They can be overly sensitive and become overwhelmed or drown in other people's passions and emotions if they don't shield properly. They may also be prone to struggles with depression. This type of "water overboard" energy can be a serious problem for some magickal people. For an immediate fix, try grounding and centering, which uses earth energy. Also, try a little sunlight therapy (for fire energy), or try the old reliable smudging technique with incense smoke, which pulls in air energy. These will help to muscle those elements back into balance quickly.

Elemental Strengths and Challenges Worksheet

Here is a worksheet where you can quickly jot down your thoughts on your magickal personality and how it relates to the four natural elements. Once you've done that, then decide which element you feel is most compatible with your character. Also note which element or elements you feel aren't well-suited to your personality. Finally, there is a space provided for you to note any elemental challenges that you may be experiencing. Once you've completed the worksheet, use it as a tool for personal change.

	My Strengths	My Challenges
Earth		
Air		
Fire		
Water		

For the elemental creatures go
About my table to and fro,
That hurry from unmeasured mind
To rant and rage in flood and wind …
WILLIAM BUTLER YEATS

PERSONAL POWER AND ELEMENTAL BLOCKS

So, what did you discover about yourself? Did you get the outcome you expected? Which element is the one you feel the least attracted to? Perhaps you should consider that you are experiencing a block in your personal power with regards to a particular element. There is nothing more frustrating for creative people than a block. And before you think, "Well, I don't consider myself artsy or creative," consider this: magicians and Witches are creative people because they create change. All magick seeks to transform or change a situation or an outcome. That's the essence of why we cast spells and work to raise our levels of personal power—because we are all working to create positive manifestations of change with our magick.

Now, personal power can become blocked for a variety of reasons. When it does, you can either whine, sulk, or mope about it, or you can take a ruthless personal inventory. Then you go to work to transform the problem into a magickal lesson and a personal strength. (Oh, and in case you are wondering—I have done all of the above. Once I was finished feeling out of sorts and frustrated, I turned the elemental blockage around and gained a better understanding of myself in the process.)

Furthermore, I discovered an important magickal lesson: in order to be an adept practitioner, your personality must be balanced with all four natural elements. It's not enough to just assume they are. Perform a bit of personal magick and pull those elements into balance. This way, your magick will flow, and you will get better results with your spellcasting.

ELEMENTAL BLOCKS—WHO, ME?

Even the best of us occasionally find our personal power low or face elemental blocks. The reason for it may come from several different sources: everyday stress, a change in your routine, moving, a different job, having a cold or recovering from an illness, family squabbles, relationship troubles, or even post-holiday blues can make us feel out of sync and disconnected from our magick, which makes it more difficult to access our personal power.

Not everyone is a perfect balance of the elements; it is normal to have more personality traits from one element than the others. It is true that invariably one of the four elements will call to you more than the others. That's to be expected. The trick is to take a hard look at your personality and how you work your magick. Then make the effort to put all four of those elements, and all their enchanting qualities, into a better working balance.

So, how do you know if you are experiencing a block in regards to your personal power? Check out the following symptoms.

Earth Block

This element corresponds to physical reality, such as wealth, health, and your personal belongings. The financial side of an earth block is a tough one for everyone, since money relates to survival. We all have concerns in this department, and no one likes the thought of being in a tough financial situation. Symptoms of an earth block are when you hold on to items or possessions that are unnecessary or disruptive to your goals, like having trouble sticking to a budget because you never can resist a sale or are going out to eat all the time. Resistance to change is another trait. When you disconnect from your physical senses and stop paying attention to your body or taking care of your health is another. If you have trouble being grounded, responsible, or dependable, these are classic earth block symptoms. A good start for you would be to consider releasing your old habits. Accept that everything is in a constant state of flux. Change is a positive thing, and it will allow you many new opportunities.

Air Block

Symptoms of an air block may be that you are holding on to old ideas or outdated beliefs that no longer serve you. Your creativity fizzles out and concentration becomes difficult. A classic example would be writer's block (shudder). The element of air embraces mental powers, intuition, and your creative ideas and concepts, for when you believe in something you are giving it life and creating the power that it has. So an air block can be one of the most frustrating blocks to work through, since this element represents your mind. This is especially troublesome as the down-and-dirty definition of magick is "mind over matter." What can you do? Distract yourself with other physical projects.

Take a walk and enjoy nature, which is linked to the element of earth. Try igniting a little fire energy and make love, or link into the element of water and go for a swim. Bottom line: distract yourself, turn off your brain, and stop thinking so damn hard! Take a break, and allow the inspiration to flow back into your life in its own way and time, without any expectations attached to it.

Fire Block

A sign of a fire block is not having enough energy and passion to complete your goals—basically that you feel as though you have lost your spunk and spark, and that you can't get fired up or enthusiastic about projects or events that once delighted you. Should you find yourself wondering what ever happened to your sexuality, you definitely have a fire block. If working to create those positive changes all seems like "too much trouble or work," you are again dealing with a fire block. Both on a personal and a magickal level, this is exasperating. Fire is the element of transformation, and if you are blocked here, you will find it difficult to transform your wishes into reality. Are you holding on to old hurt feelings and unresolved issues? It's time to shed some light on the problems. A prescription for you to consider is to do something constructive, like exercise, and to release your anger in a affirmative way. If you feel disconnected from your sexuality, then do something positive just for you—something that will transform your self-image and make you feel better about yourself. Whether you are male or female, you can change your look, get a new haircut, color your hair, try different body care products or a new personal scent. Buy new sexy underwear or a whole outfit. Treat yourself to a massage. Get a baby sitter and take your partner out for an evening of romance. Use your imagination, and you'll get those juices flowing again.

Water Block

The sign of a water block is emotional turmoil. Since the element of water classically represents emotions, this can be an especially uncomfortable block. Here we are dealing with the more negative emotions, such as sadness and anger. Now it's certainly true that none of us likes to admit when we are behaving badly. But being pent-up emotionally is the equivalent of a being a walking, ticking time bomb. Eventually all that anger and emotional frustration will spill over—and probably at a socially inappropriate time. These emotions may run deep. But unless you take a hard look at why you feel it's so important to repress the feelings and hold on to them, you won't move forward. Study those murky emotions, climb out of that swirling pool of hurt, and start to release that frustration in healthy ways. Claim your emotions, and admit when you are upset or your feelings are hurt. Have a nice cry, and then wash your face and start dealing with the issues. Try journaling. Or you can have a little chat with a friend or partner—that's a positive talk, by the way, not a shouting contest—and clear things up. If this isn't an option, then consider finding a therapist and talking about your troubles. Therapy can be a positive tool for change. Don't dismiss the idea.

REMOVING ELEMENTAL BLOCKS

Probably you will discover that you have a combination of the above blockages. And if so, you've got work to do, my friend. This situation calls for soul-searching, some personal transformation, and then banishing those elemental blocks. This will probably be some of the most challenging spellwork you will face, for many reasons. First off, it's very personal, and your fears and emotions are involved. It's tough to let go of fear of failure, frustration, old ideas, or unhealthy habits. But this type of purge is a positive step and can become a powerful tool for self-transformation.

I know that when I faced a blockage to my personal power there were a few of the elements involved. Which ones did I have blocked? Okay, I'll give. They were air and fire. I had way too much water energy and earth energy, and they had smothered the other two. So did I figure this out all by my amazing little witchy self? No, I had a talk with a dear friend, and she gently pointed out that I needed to take a closer look at my personal energies and see if I was experiencing a block. Actually, she gave me a "mom" type of lecture, which was the magickal equivalent of getting a loving *whack!* upside the head.

But you know, once I really thought about her suggestions, I was able to figure out what the problem was. Then I rolled up my sleeves and worked to put those elements back in balance. I felt so much better afterwards, lighter and clearer-headed. My family and other friends noticed a change in my attitude as well. But I worked damn hard on pulling myself and my personal energies back in line.

You can't just announce, "Oh, I have some unresolved anger. I have a fire block," and *poof!* problem solved. Nope, it takes a few steps. First you've got to sit down and figure out what started the block. Second, admit the problem. Third, work through the emotions that go along with the issue. Finally, work magick to pull things back in line.

Hey, we all go through tough times, and then our personal power and magick goes out of whack. The tough part is working through all those steps. It takes time and perseverance. Don't beat yourself up emotionally about it either. Blocks and imbalances happen to all of us. So suck it up, figure out what the problem is, start to make the necessary personal changes, and then get to work. Challenging? You betcha. But I'll wager that you are more than up to the task. The following is a ritual that I designed when I faced down my own elemental blocks.

A Ritual to Pull those Elements Back in Line

Timing and Directions

To banish those blocks and obstructions, work in harmony with the waning lunar cycle. Try a Monday to add extra lunar power or a Saturday to bring in the closing energies of the week and the protective powers of Saturn.

Supplies and Directions

Gather together a copy of the worksheet on page 62 and a simple natural representation of each of the four elements, such as a feather for air, a seashell for water, a crystal for earth, and a white tealight candle for fire. Finally, set the tealight in a holder, and arrange the other components around it. Light the candle, take a few moments to focus on the elemental blocks that are obstructing your personal power, and then repeat the opening verse:

> *Come earth, fire, water, and wind,*
> *Not to break but only to mend.*
> *Pull the four elements in line equal and true,*
> *Bring harmony and balance to all that I do.*

Next, take the copy of your elemental worksheet, and read over what you have discovered about yourself. Take a few more moments to meditate and consider all the personal work you have already done to bring the elements back into a harmonious, working balance.

When you feel ready, continue with these lines:

> By the elements earth, air, fire, and water,
>
> I will remove all blocks and reclaim my power.
>
> Now, remove all doubt, negativity, and fear.
>
> I ask that the path to my goals be gently cleared.

Allow the candle to burn in a safe place until it goes out on its own. Ground and center, and then close the ritual with the following lines:

> By all the powers of land and sea,
>
> As I do will it, so mote it be.

Now that you've started the process of pulling the elements into balance and removing any blocks, let's discuss ways to raise and work with your personal power.

While with an eye made quiet by the power

of harmony and the deep power of joy,

we see into the life of things.

WILLIAM WORDSWORTH

FINDING AND RAISING POWER
THE NATURAL WAY

Ooh, I said the magick word, didn't I? *Power.* There's the ultimate goal that captures people's attention and makes us search and study like crazy to gain this elusive quality.

As we've seen, magickal power comes from the elements and the constantly changing energies of the moon, sun, and stars. It grows from nature, and springs from deep inside of you. Everyone's personal power is as distinctive as a fingerprint. We are not all like little witchy cookies cut out of the same mold. Honestly, power is a funny thing. You either carry it or you don't. Here's another big surprise: no one can give you power and you don't "take it" from someone else either. Power is naturally in everything, and it is everywhere. This energy is literally a force of nature. The trick is to identify it—and to coax it into working harmoniously with you (which we have been diligently working on in this chapter). So celebrate this, and be proud of your individuality! It is important to recognize that each of us will find our power and direct it in our own way.

Here the heart may give a useful lesson to the head,

and Learning wiser grow without his books.

WILLIAM COWPER

LESSONS LEARNED

I have a story I'd like to share with you. I think it will help you to understand and to remember a few important magickal lessons. Also, it will probably make you chuckle. Many years ago when I attended an intermediate class on Wicca, the leaders of the class asked us all to get up and to demonstrate our circlecasting abilities, one by one. Now, if memory serves, this class topic was on circlecastings—so I was surprised the class started off with this magickal show-and-tell instead of a lecture.

I watched with interest as the other students took their turns. Everyone seemed to be casting their circles in a similar fashion, but that didn't surprise me. They had all just taken a Wicca 101 class together. Only myself and a man were the new students here. As my turn rolled around, I stood up, walked to the center of the room, and closed my eyes. I silently asked the elements to lend their power to mine and began turning in a slow clockwise circle, stopping at each quarter. As I made my way around the circle, I pointed my finger to the ground and visualized a blue circle of flame running along the ground, totally surrounding me. I finished up, centered, and opened my eyes to look at the teachers.

The teachers seemed miffed, and a few members of the class were staring at me like I'd suddenly grown two heads. Embarrassed, I fell back on my best defense: attitude. "What?" I demanded.

"That's a lot of power to just be tossing around." One of the teachers looked at me like I'd committed a horrible crime.

"You told us to show you how we cast a circle," I said carefully.

"What energy are you using?" the first teacher asked suspiciously.

"Well, basically, I am using my own, along with—" I began.

"No, no, no, dear." The first teacher interrupted and proceeded to look down her nose. "You *never* use your own power, and where are your gestures?"

She hadn't picked anyone else's performance apart ... so how come I was so lucky?

"My what?" I asked.

At this point, the second teacher let loose a deeply annoyed sigh, accompanied by an eye roll. "Your *gestures*. Your salutes at each quarter."

Jeez, they didn't have to be so snotty about it. "I suppose I am just a gesture-free kind of Witch," I shot back with a grin, thinking immediately of one hand gesture I'd love to show both these teachers.

The request had been to show them how each individual would cast a circle. And hey, my circlecasting always worked for me. Who were they to tell me I was "wrong"? It was a nasty surprise to get up, do my thing, and then get harshly critiqued in front of the rest of the group. Thoroughly embarrassed and offended, I sat down so the next victim—I mean student—could nervously take their turn.

As I sat back down, a fellow classmate, the only other new person, leaned over, put his hand on my arm, and whispered to me. "You did fine. I think you really surprised them. So, you're a natural Witch, right?" Laughing softly at my stunned expression, he patted my arm in support. "You just called on the elements in your head." He made that last bit a statement.

Wow. How did he know that? "Yes, I asked them to lend their power to mine," I admitted. Now I was very intrigued. He was in the Order of Bards Ovates and Druids … maybe his knowing was a Druid thing.

"Thought so." He grinned at me. "I could feel them in the room. Girl, you raised the hair off my neck."

When it was his turn, he also cast a circle silently and without any hand gestures. The difference between his circlecasting and mine was that he moved around with a sort of grace that reminded me of martial arts.

Well, I thought to myself, *isn't that interesting how our techniques are so similar?* It was simply awesome to experience, and it was the first time I ever felt someone else's power radiate out in a room. Impressed, I looked at him with new eyes, as the importance of this discovery about personal magickal power hit me like a ton of bricks.

Raising magickal power has nothing to do with your magickal tradition, fancy words, or grandiose gestures. Power comes from within (the heart and mind), and it comes from without (the four elements, nature, and the sun, moon, and stars). Whatever witchy flair or positive personal spin you choose to put on this is perfectly fine.

The idea here is to focus on how you raise and direct power, and how you interact with the four natural elements and the magick. Everyone has the right to express themselves differently with magick. This is something I call "magick with personality." So be yourself. That distinctiveness and individuality add something special and extraordinary to your magick.

Skill comes from practice.

Chinese proverb

Practice makes Perfect: An Energy Ball Exercise to Raise Power and to Focus Your Intuition

Here is an exercise that helps students learn to raise power, to sense it, and to practice moving energy around. This exercise will help you tune in to your intuition and psychic centers, and teach you how to focus your personal power. Plus this is also a great ice-breaker and a wonderful way to help a class, circle, or coven get to know each other better. For this exercise, you will need a partner, a pen, and some paper to take notes on.

First, you'll both need to ground and center yourselves. For this exercise, you and your partner should sit on the ground and face each other. Then focus your power at the solar plexus area (just under the rib cage and above the navel). Tighten up those muscles and envision a bright yellow ball of energy there. Now one person begins to build an energy ball by raising and shaping their personal power.

Start by briskly rubbing your hands together. As soon as you feel your palms grow warm, slowly begin to pull your hands apart a few inches. You will feel some resistance, as if you were pulling taffy. Shape and mold the energy into a ball. The approximate size of the energy ball will vary, but think tennis ball or softball size.

Your next step is to program the energy ball with something positive. Since you are passing this to another, it has to be positive and enjoyable. It would be spiteful to fill an energy ball full of stress or anger, so you need to promise that you won't build anything that you wouldn't like to receive yourself! Visualize what lovely thing you want the ball to become. Some simple and elemental suggestions are twirling green ivy leaves, gossamer and multicolored fluttering butterflies, cool, blue waves of water, or warm, dancing flames.

Try other themes from nature, too, such as red rose petals, yellow daisies, white clouds, shining stars in a nighttime sky, etc. Just pick an upbeat and fun image—even something as simple as swirling pink paper hearts would be fine—as long as it is a positive image you feel that you can load into the energy ball easily.

Now that it's loaded, pass it to your partner. Once they have it in their hands, turn away and write down a few keywords, then tuck the paper out of sight. Give your partner a few moments to sense it. When on the receiving end of an energy ball, keep these points in mind:

- Go with your first impressions—don't overthink the process.
- Close your eyes as you sense the energy ball. (That forces you to gather impressions through your psychic senses instead of your physical ones.)

- You may find it helpful to focus on your third eye area (center of the forehead or the solar plexus), where your intuitive centers rest.

At this point, the recipient has the option of passing the energy ball back, taking it inside themselves, or giving it/ grounding it back to the earth. If they pass it back, the builder may then ground it in the earth. If the recipient chooses to keep it, they should simply press their hands to their chest, absorbing the energy. Lastly, if they wish, they may turn their hands over and give it back to the earth.

Now the receiver tells the builder what their impressions were. The builder should take out their notes so they can compare what the other picked up on. Finally, both the builder and the receiver should ground and center. Then switch roles. The recipient becomes the builder, and vice versa.

Once you get things rolling, see what results you get from mixing things up. Keep the pace quick, and if you are working with a group, have everyone switch partners and begin the exercise again. I have noticed over the years that sometimes established couples do wonderfully together. They can be impressive to watch. Since they already have a bond of emotion, they can be very quick to catch on and tune in. And then sometimes they just butt heads. So keep people switching around and the atmosphere light. This is a fun and quick psychic exercise; it doesn't take long. It makes people laugh, learn to build power, sense energy, and trust their own intuitive abilities. Plus, it really gets the group in a great positive mood.

Keep the energy ball images upbeat and happy. That way, everyone has a fun experience. Also, first impressions are usually the most accurate. So go with the flow, trust your intuition, and see what you discover.

❧

First impressions are often the truest . . .

WILLIAM HAZLITT

❧

TRUSTING THOSE FIRST IMPRESSIONS

Recently, I had one student partnered up with her husband for this exercise. These two were acquaintances of mine; they were recently married, and she was very nervous. The husband had a dominant personality, and she was a sweet girl, but a little naïve. She became frustrated with the exercise very quickly. She looked over at me from where she sat on the floor facing her husband and started whining, "I can't do it!"

The husband began making soothing noises and hushed her immediately. He then told her that because he was so powerful with energy manipulation, this was the reason she couldn't pick up any information. (Which, as you already guessed, is a huge contradiction.) The whole class looked over at them in amazement, and a few people chuckled. If he was as powerful as he claimed, then it ought to have been a snap.

Surprised at his behavior and his condescending attitude toward her, I bristled. About a dozen rude comments ran through my head as I heroically fought against the urge to go and smack him upside the head.

So I settled for a different option. Being the gentle, patient soul that I am, I quickly stepped in and firmly grabbed her hands. I pulled her up off the floor and led her over to the opposite side of the room, well away from where her husband was sitting.

I explained that this time I would build the energy ball and she would receive it. It was up to her what she did with it after she "looked it over" and sensed it. She could hand it back, take it inside, or give it back to the earth. It was her choice, and no matter what, I wouldn't be offended.

Quickly, I built an energy ball between my hands. In my mind, I envisioned it as being a ball of fluffy white clouds, soft, free floating, and soothing. I handed it to her, and her face went soft. I turned away and quickly wrote down what I had envisioned, then turned back to her. After a moment, she began to frown. "I can't get it," she complained.

"You are thinking too hard," I said and then suggested, "What were your first impressions? What words or pictures came into your mind immediately?"

"Oh." Her shoulders dropped and she relaxed and pulled the energy ball into her chest. She stood there a moment, humming softly, and then smiled beautifully. "It was soft, fluffy, and warm … like white cotton balls."

I laughed and handed her the paper where I had written down what I had envisioned when I built the energy ball: *white, fluffy, and floating clouds.*

"I did it!" She was thrilled.

"See?" I said to her. "You can do it. You just need to believe in your own power, and trust those first impressions." She walked back to stand next to her husband, who immediately started to critique her first attempts. She looked up at him and sweetly told him to shut up. Which he did.

I hid a laugh with a cough.

Personality is the supreme realization of the innate
idiosyncrasy of a living being. It is an act of high
courage flung in the face of life, the absolute
affirmation of all that constitutes
the individual . . .

CARL JUNG

YOU'VE GOT PERSONALITY

Personal power is the key to your magickal experiences. Now that you have worked your way through this chapter, you have learned a little bit more about yourself and grown along the way. Sometimes to become a more powerful magickal person, we need to embrace who we are, become happy with our individuality, and learn to laugh at ourselves and to gain knowledge from life as we go along.

Effective personal power occurs when you tap into the elements, use your creativity, and then allow yourself to enjoy its benefits. Personal power that is balanced can strongly influence your life, and other people will be drawn to you and influenced within their own free wills by that positive force. Applying personal power to your daily life is an exercise in free will. You have the choice to create and to experience all the positive changes that you dream of.

Embrace your personal strengths, work to balance out any weaknesses, and watch for the positive changes that will manifest in your life. The tools for transformation are within your own two hands and within your heart. Celebrate your individuality, style, and personality. If you are willing to work hard and to believe in yourself, then nothing will be impossible for you.

Chapter 4

Personal change, growth, development, identity
formation—these tasks that once were thought
to belong to childhood and adolescence alone
now are recognized as part of adult life as well.

LILLIAN BRESLOW RUBIN

Personal Magickal Development

In the past chapters, we have discussed intuition, psychic ability, and personal power. This has been a preparation of sorts to bring us to where we are at this point of the book: working on your personal magickal development. I have yet to meet a Witch who wasn't interested in expanding their comprehension of the Craft. How many of you have searched and studied, but wondered what happened to that amazing rush that you felt when you first began to practice? Is it gone forever, or have you simply grown out of the excitement of new magickal discoveries?

Have you considered that the answer may lie within and not without? And yes, that is a direct reference to the Charge of the Goddess. All that you have ever really needed to create magick in your life is already within your grasp. There is a reason that experienced Witches encourage other magickal practitioners to look inside themselves and to work on their own personal development. So much of magick depends on your strength of character and your own level of perception and sensitivity. The only way you can learn more about those aspects is to look within and do a little soul-searching. Being a natural Witch and working on your individual development can be an amazing journey. This gives you the opportunity to follow your own heart, listen to your intuitions, and flex your personal power; best of all, it provides the chance to learn and to grow.

> *The whole of science is nothing more than*
> *a refinement of everyday thinking.*
> ALBERT EINSTEIN

EVERYDAY WITCHERY

Making the decision to expand your magick and to practice the art and science of your craft every day requires commitment and motivation. How do you stay motivated? One way is to celebrate your witchery every day. To start, try thinking as a natural Witch might—which is to observe, note, and celebrate the seasons as they change.

There is more to the Wheel of the Year than just celebrating the eight sabbats. Some individuals find the process of dragging out all their ritual tools and supplies so daunting that they don't even bother to celebrate the holidays anymore. They lose their connection because they are overwhelmed by the mechanics, and they are missing the whole point. Keep your celebrations simple and be spontaneous. It's not about which book you pull your rituals from or what accessories you own. It's about your connection to nature.

May I ask you a personal question? When was the last time you splashed around in a puddle, walked in the rain, or watched a robin build a nest? And don't give me the argument that you live in the city. Here is your perfect excuse to go to the park or check out the trees in the neighborhood. Come on, live on the edge and go for a walk outside.

I'd like to remind you to get all your senses involved, and to find and experience that connection to nature. Take a jog through the park on a pleasant day. Go ahead, build a sand castle on the beach, or walk through the surf at sunset and hunt for seashells. Watch a thunderstorm roll through your town. Stroll through a lush summer garden. Feel the seasonal energies that are swirling around you. Kick through some falling autumn leaves. Breathe deep and smell that cooling evening air! What scents do you associate with each season? Go for a walk around the block during a snowfall and throw a few snowballs, or watch the icicles drip. Fill up a bird feeder for those winter birds, and enjoy the show. Just find simple ways to enjoy nature, no matter where you live or what the season.

Sensing the Energies of the Seasons

Have you ever tuned in to your intuition and noticed what different psychic energies are available to you during each of the four quarters of the year? Or are you too busy cursing at the weather and finding the whole thing a general inconvenience to your daily schedule? Yes, it is certainly easier to rhapsodize over a gorgeous spring day or a lovely autumn evening. But the seasons and their cycles each bring their own magick.

For example, this past winter was a gloomy one. It was on the dry side, and we didn't get very much snow. We did, however, get more than our fair share of days when it was overcast, windy, and cold. Occasionally we would get a tease of spring, where milder temperatures prevailed. But the sporadic mild winter weather did make me appreciate the break in the temperatures. One late winter afternoon, I took advantage of the break and managed to sneak in some winter gardening. As the temperatures had hovered in the forties for a few days with a bit of rain, the ground was soft, and I was even able to get that last renegade bag of pink tulip bulbs planted.

It was muddy and chilly outside, and the gardens did not look especially pretty while I dug around. But the scent of the fresh-turned earth and the fragrance of last year's fallen leaves were bracing. That day, I simply ignored the mud and felt my spirits lift. As I pulled back fallen leaves to dig the holes for my tulip bulbs, I discovered the earliest of the bright green shoots of my daffodils just breaking the ground. As I carefully dug around my other sleeping perennials, I made sure to cover back up those tender spears as I planted my tulip bulbs.

My husband walked outside to find me gently reminding the daffodils that we still had a ways to go before spring and to not be fooled by a midwinter thaw. When he asked what I was doing, I pulled back the leaves to show him the hints of spring green. His reaction was the same as mine had been—a big smile.

The halfway point between winter and spring, Imbolc, was only days away, and here was a physical reminder for both of us that the Wheel of the Year was indeed turning. And the two of us stayed there for a while, hunkered down next to the winter-dormant perennial beds, making sure the fallen autumn leaves were patted snugly back down to protect those shoots.

It was an excellent reminder for me that while that particular time of the year may not be especially pretty in the garden, there is still magick happening and plenty of natural energies to sense. Just remembering what it felt like to get in a bit of unexpected winter gardening cheered me right up. Plus knowing that the daffodils were waiting—not too patiently—to pop up and to welcome back the spring in another six weeks didn't hurt either.

The trees and plants were still dormant, but change was coming. You could feel it in the air and sense it when you placed your hands on that water-logged garden soil. There had been a sleepy sort of vibe to nature at that time. But I was reminded on that midwinter afternoon that underneath those fallen leaves and brown grass, nature was just beginning to stir—and that was a creative type of energy that I could certainly put to good use in my magick.

> *The sweet-souled Poet of the Seasons stood listening,*
> *and listening long, in rapturous mood . . .*
> WILLIAM WORDSWORTH

PSYCHIC ENERGIES OF THE SEASONS

Here are the themes I have always found to work well with the four seasons. Experiment with these for yourself, and see what you can discover. In the winter months, we traditionally want to stay indoors and snuggle up, and our intuition leads us into looking within and personal introspection. In the springtime, we feel the need to shake ourselves off and to do something creative. We are motivated and full of new, fresh energy, hope, and ideas for the year. During the summer months, the tempo slows a bit, and we are influenced by the heat of the day and those sultry evenings. In the autumn months, the inner focus shifts to a personal harvest—what we have learned all year and how we will put this all to practice.

Discovering these intuitive energies and psychic cycles for yourself is an excellent way to expand your magickal abilities. It also gives you an opportunity to design and live your own personal magickal tradition. If you want to understand the nature of magick, you have to be attuned to her seasons, for the most intuitive Witches know that in order to work harmoniously with the earth's energies, they need to be in step with the planetary rhythms and seasons of the earth. What follows are a few ideas to help you develop that intuitive connection.

SEASONAL SPELLS

This time I thought we would mix things up a bit—instead of the usual spell candle setup, I decided it would be more interesting to work with the aroma lamps that are often used in aromatherapy. These small ceramic dishes are inexpensive and easily found in candle shops or arts and crafts stores. I picked one up for about five dollars. I have a friend who is an aromatherapist, and she uses these little lamps often. She asked me why I never wrote spells that included these handy little lamps, and the more I thought about it, the better I liked the idea.

After all, as she pointed out, the four elements are all represented neatly. The lamp itself is typically made of ceramic material (representing earth). The small tealight that is placed inside represents fire when it is lit. There is water that sits in the dish above, and the fragrant essential oils that you drop into the water are for the element of air.

As the water heats up from the candle below, the scent is released into the room, and scent is one of our most powerful senses. It evokes strong memories and affects the magickal mood. Certain scents can affect your psychic centers and your awareness on a subtle level. They do this as the magickally charged aroma filters into the body, and this, in turn, creates a change in your conscious and psychic mind.

Supplies

- An aroma lamp
- Plain, unscented tealight candles (most tealight candles burn for approximately four hours)
- Essential oils (use the suggested seasonal scent or choose your own)
- A lighter or matches
- A safe, flat surface to set up on
- Other items as desired to personalize the spell

A Note for Personalizing

You may wish to personalize these seasonal spells; that is completely up to you. But if the idea gets your Witch's imagination running, here are just a few quick ideas you can try: scatter metallic star confetti on the work surface and around the lamp. Add a snip or two of fresh pine, or arrange seashells, stones, flower petals or even colorful autumn leaves on the work surface. (Be sure to keep flammable items well away from the tealight and the lamp, of course. That ceramic dish does heat up!) If you live in the tropics, Deep South, or desert Southwest, obviously you might wish to incorporate natural items and plants that are local to you during the various seasons. So improvise and adapt. Don't be bashful about putting your own spin on these seasonal spells! Also, you may refer to the Book of Witchery located in the back of this book for even more magickal essential oils to work with.

Witchery tip: don't go crazy on the oil. You can always add more. The first time I tried it, I added several drops of essential oil to the water, and it was very strong. My entire house was scented in only twenty-five minutes from one little aroma lamp. I was surprised at how powerful the scent was when it heated through. So I blew out the candle, let the ceramic dish cool off, and dumped out the water and oil. My second attempt was much better, as I just added two drops of essential oil to the water.

Directions

To begin, set the aroma lamp in a safe place away from small children or curious pets. Slip the tealight candle into the bottom section and then add two tablespoons of water to the dish. Choose the essential oil that coordinates with the season and the goal, and add a drop or two to the water.

As the oil hits the water, begin the spell by saying,

> *Now this natural oil so fair*
> *Adds psychic power to the air.*

Recap the vial of the essential oil and set aside. Light the tealight candle. While you put the essential oil away, allow the water to heat up and the scent to start diffusing within the room. It takes about three to five minutes. Once you can smell the aroma and know that it is indeed releasing its fragrance into your environment, then repeat the spell verse. Afterwards you can meditate for a while, or relax and take notes in the journal space that is provided in the back of this book. Jot down what your intuition tells you and what your feelings were. Lastly, note how your intuitive spells manifested.

Winter: Intuitive Spell for Introspection

Scent—sandalwood or frankincense. These scents encourage spirituality and meditation, which are perfect for this season's theme of introspection.

> *As the cold winter winds do blow and spin,*
>
> *I now focus my attention within.*
>
> *Introspection is the key at this time of the year;*
>
> *My future aspirations will become bright and clear.*

Spring: Intuitive Spell for Motivation

Scent—neroli or sweet orange. These sweet fragrances promote purification, energy, and joy. These fragrances should help get you revitalized and ready for all the growth and change spring can bring.

> *During this season of rebirth and the spring,*
>
> *Motivation and courage to me now bring.*
>
> *I call for the powers of growth and success,*
>
> *May my magickal workings be truly blessed.*

Summer: Intuitive Spell for Passion for Your Path

Scent—ylang ylang or rose. These heady and luscious summertime scents promote loving vibrations and passion for your personal development, and can soothe and calm any atmosphere. They are just the thing for a sultry summer day or night.

I call on the strength and energy of the sun

To light my way clearly, bringing passion and fun.

I will travel this old path with strength, truth, and grace,

May purpose and honor walk with me all my days.

Fall: Intuitive Spell for Harvesting Knowledge

Scent—patchouli or oak moss. These autumn scents are earthy and musky. They promote prosperity, abundance, and higher personal energy.

During the harvesttide, the autumn leaves will turn.

I offer thanks for the many lessons I've learned.

May I use this power in wise and wonderful ways.

With wisdom and knowledge, I face the darkening days.

Closing the Intuitive Seasonal Spells

Allow the tealight to burn until it is gone or until the water has evaporated. When that happens, you may close the spell by saying:

For inner knowledge true, bringing harm to none,

By fire and scent, this psychic spell is done.

Once the lamp has cooled to the touch, carefully wipe out the oil dish so your lamp is ready to go for the next spell.

Remember to focus on and to enjoy the seasons every day, no matter what zone you live in. Stay connected to the natural world as the year turns, and you will discover a new level of perception. Now use this knowledge wisely, and add it to your own personal magickal traditions; for the more we work with and empathize with the seasons and cycles of nature, the more we develop spiritually.

Sensing Your Own Magick

Occasionally someone will toss a question my way about sensing or seeing the manifestations of their own magick. A good example of this is when folks cast a magickal circle and then wonder why they don't see a blue circle of flame along the ground. All the books say that they are supposed to visualize a circle of light, so they start to wonder where in the world it is. It's a fair question, and I think that many times we all sort of hold our breath and wait for some type of movie special effect when it comes to magick and spellcasting.

Nope, your candle flames aren't going to spontaneously combust into light, and objects won't float about the room while you cast your spells and charms. So how do you really know when your magick is taking hold? You will know by paying attention to your intuition and by noticing the physical sensations your body gives you.

It's a very rare Witch indeed that can see visual manifestations of their magick every time. I am sure that someone who is, let's say, talented in seeing auras could probably make out a circle of light on the ground, but for many of us, that's not going to happen. This does not mean that there is anything wrong with you, nor are you doing anything incorrectly. It's all about your perception level and how the individual Witch experiences their own magick, which ties right back to our opening chapters and your psychic perception levels. (You just knew I was going to link this all back together, didn't you?)

For example, when you cast a circle, you'll need to experiment and see what works best for you and how your own body reacts to the energy that is present. You may have to visualize or imagine that circle of light, seeing it in your mind's eye, for instance. In the physical world, things may not look any different, but on the astral plane—the level where magick lives—that circle is really there. So don't be disappointed in what you experience. Instead, use this fact as an exercise in which you can develop, understand, and appreciate your own magickal perception levels.

It's far more likely that you are a Witch who physically senses their magick. Next time you cast your circle, walk the perimeter. Then purposely step out of your circle—across the boundary, wait a moment—and then step back in. Did you feel anything different? How did your solar plexus feel? I know that for myself I feel a tightening and a tug at that region when I cross the boundary of a magickal circle. (Which doesn't surprise me, as this is the seat of the empath's power.) I have had circle mates describe a sensation of a mild tightening of the chest or throat, accompanied by a little shift in their emotions. It's not uncomfortable, but they do notice it. (Which links back into a psychic intuitive's reactions to energy and magick.) Do you imagine that a Witch who senses a physical reaction to a circle is less attuned to their surroundings than, say, someone who can "see" the energy? Absolutely not. These types of perceptions are only different, and one is not better than the other.

So you'll need to experiment and ask yourself, while inside of your cast circle, do you feel warmer—or cooler? How about when you stepped back and forth over the boundary of your circle? Did it give you a tingle, or did your stomach flip? Did crossing back and forth raise goose bumps? All of these sensations and about a dozen more are possible. Whip out your notebook, and write down what you physically feel. What are those psychic senses telling you? How did your body react? Pay attention and see what those reactions can teach you about your own perception levels.

Remember that magick is as individual as a fingerprint, and so too are your physical reactions to it. You can truly do anything you set your mind to. There is a reason we say, "As you will it, then so shall it be." Don't focus on what you *think* you don't know—instead, focus on what you are discovering!

ETHICS: A PERSONAL DECISION

As you are increasing your skills and comprehension of magick, ethics takes on a more important role than ever before. A good mental image to keep in mind is that the magickal universe is like the shimmering strands of a spider's web. It is beautiful, intricate, and interwoven in a fascinating pattern. As everything in nature is interconnected, if you should happen to touch one part of this cosmic web, the whole web of life vibrates. Performing affirmative magick and casting spells and charms to bring about positive change is one way to weave a new design into the spiritual web. For Witches and Wiccans, this is an important visualization, because working any magick is a lesson in cause and effect.

So you should consider how your wishes will affect the overall design. Is your magick a wise use of your personal power? Does it honor the connection that all living things share? Magick at its most basic level is performed to transform situations into the best possible outcome for all those involved. Affirmative magick does not stir up chaos, bring heartache to others, or coerce; this goes against the very nature of positive change. Free will is vital, and magickal manipulation can be considered a negative use of your personal power.

Manipulation:
What It Is and How to Avoid It

Manipulation may be defined as "to control or play upon another by an artful or insidious means to one's own advantage." In other words: tampering with another person's free will. A classic example would be a love spell cast on an unknowing target. However, manipulation typically occurs in magick by accident, even by practitioners who start out with good intentions.

Healing spells cast without the intended's permission are a common and unknowing example of magickal manipulation. Yes, of course you want to help, and healing is indeed a positive magick. However, working without permission means that you are manipulating the situation and person for what *you* want. This, unfortunately, may not be the best thing for the patient. The easiest fix for this scenario? Speak up. Inquire if you can send some energy to them or just ask bluntly if you could perform a spell to help the individual regain their health. Problem solved.

Manipulation can also easily occur when casting to fix a problem with your job or when going for a promotion at work. Think before you start casting. When in doubt, work magick on yourself only, not that so-and-so is seen for the numbskull they are. I have heard all sorts of war stories over the years about this. Recently I sat in dismay as an individual bragged to a large mixed magickal-tradition group about a job-related spell they had once cast.

This storyteller had cast their spell so an annoying coworker would be seen for who they really were. Supposedly the other person was a thorn in the side of the whole office. Seems they were always running around and overseeing everyone else, but in reality they themselves did very little. Once the magick was cast (and the caster had mixed their deities and techniques with all the subtlety of a high-speed blender), the target of the spell began having major problems at work. Their job performance was called into question within a week. Eventually the victim of the spell became such an emotional wreck that they were reprimanded for poor performance, suffered an emotional breakdown, and were ultimately fired.

The caster, now enjoying a better position since that other employee was gone, didn't seem to clue in that they had just indulged in manipulative and cruel magick. They had indeed caused emotional harm, just because they wanted to.

But the other folks who were listening in dove on the topic as soon as the storyteller was out of earshot. The general take on it by the Witches, Pagans, and Wiccans all present was that it was a nasty and exploitative spell, full of abuse, cruelty, and spite. Plus it fit the classic definition of manipulation, which is playing upon another by insidious means to one's own advantage. And isn't it interesting that everyone present was horrified, no matter what their beliefs and practices?

Maybe we—as Wiccans and Witches, traditionalists and eclectics—have much more in common than we realize. Here's a thought: as a community of conscientious practitioners, we should celebrate our similarities, honors, and strengths, and not pick at each other quite so much.

Nobody ever said that expanding your magickal skills was going to be quick and easy. It takes a lot of commitment and practice. But guess what? Magick requires effort. Remember that your magick should create harmony and a positive change within the overall spiritual design of your life.

You need to be both careful and conscientious if you're going to cast spells and perform magick. Just because you carry power doesn't mean you should be zapping the bejesus out of every little situation that comes along. Self-defense is one thing; however, try to use some discretion. A sense of humor is a good idea too. Laugh at yourself and ridiculous situations in general. Look beyond the melodrama of the moment, and attempt to see the big picture. Have a little chat with the God and Goddess, and ask for their help in showing you the right course of action. Witchcraft is considered to be the Craft of the Wise, so use a bit of wisdom and your common sense, and think before you start casting. Consider that spiritual web and how your actions will affect it.

Magick works because you send out personal power loaded full of intention. It does and will return even stronger, because magick is cause and effect. You will have to take responsibility for your magickal actions. Do you want to bring happiness, harmony, and prosperity into your life? Then you must treat all other living creatures in the same manner that you wish to be treated: fairly, ethically, and with respect and compassion. In effect, you vow to be conscientious with your personal magickal power.

> *Tradition simply means that we need to end what*
> *began well, and continue what is worth continuing.*
> JOSE BERGAMIN

LEARNING AND GROWING IN THE CRAFT

While you learn and grow in the Craft, you are surely weaving your own web of magick and creating your own practices and individual traditions. You will also be making some important personal and ethical decisions. In the Craft, your right to be an individual and your decision as to how you will practice your magick is completely up to you, no matter what title or name you give yourself. There are many wise practitioners who believe the Craft isn't just about titles and degrees—those only encompass one level. If you look deeper, you discover that the Craft is, by its very nature, all about personal development and personal power.

In truth, nontraditional, eclectic practitioners and traditionalists all rely on their own integrity, sense of responsibility, and personal codes of honor. They must (and do) take responsibility for their own actions, and they make their choices based on what they consider to be moral and ethical. They do this because they believe it is the correct and ethical thing to do for themselves, no matter what their magickal practice.

This means a self-taught Witch has much more in common with a traditional Witch than they may realize. There's an interesting thought, and one that I recently learned firsthand when I had a chance to visit with a formally trained Gardnerian High Priestess, who had been practicing and teaching her craft and tradition for over thirty years. I sat in awe at her kindness, wisdom, sense of humor, and interest in my own magickal practices. I was blown away to discover that we had much in common. She was just as anxious to learn from me as I was from her. Well, can you beat that? I never would have imagined such a scenario, and it was an important personal lesson for me to learn.

Focus on your personal development, and see how you express yourself as a Witch. Whether you prefer to stay a solitary practitioner or choose to venture out in the community to find like-minded folks, always seek out the opportunities to study, grow, and experience the magick however you can. Personal development is just another way of improving or advancing your magickal skills. So get motivated, keep your eyes open for new opportunities, and see what you can learn.

Chapter 5

If you have form'd a circle to go into,

go into it yourself and see how you would do.

WILLIAM BLAKE

Starting a Circle

While I imagine that most people would visualize a natural Witch's path to be a solitary one, that is not necessarily true. There are options, and sometimes there is just no substitute for working with a group. Yes, there are plenty of Witches who prefer to work in a solitary fashion, but there are also plenty of Witches who enjoy working with others.

Benefits to working with a magickal group include the opportunity to build friendships and to learn new techniques from the other members. When you work with a group, you get the chance to stretch your wings a bit, to share your own expertise and to experience different magickal styles and methods from the other individuals. In a group setting there is a sense of fellowship and companionship, and of course when you get several people all focusing on the same goal, the magickal power and positive change they can generate is phenomenal.

So now you are all fired up and enthusiastic about the idea. And I bet you are wondering what it really does take to find a good coven or circle. Is it sheer luck that you stumble across one, or does it take more than chance? Sure, we all have an idea in mind of the "perfect" group for ourselves: a place where we are accepted without question, where everyone not only gets along but enjoys each other's company, a place where there is the atmosphere of learning, enjoyment, magick, and spiritual reverence. But how in the world do you locate such a coven, circle, or group? We can't just flip open the phone book and find a handy listing. Where's the fun in that? This presents us with yet another question to mull over: have you ever considered building your own magickal group?

> *What we have to do ... is to find a way to celebrate*
> *our diversity and debate our differences*
> *without fracturing our communities.*
> HILLARY RODHAM CLINTON

CIRCLE OR COVEN: WHAT'S THE DIFFERENCE?

If a circle is not the same as a coven, then what is it exactly? Well, frankly, a circle is not unlike a coven. However, they are subtly different. The terms "coven" and "circle" are sometimes used interchangeably, and just to keep things interesting, they can refer to two completely separate things. One is not better or more desirable than the other; they are simply different, and they each have their place within the magickal community.

Historically a coven is a group of twelve Witches that is led by a priest or priestess, bringing their number to thirteen. (To be fair, these days the number of members can vary widely.) A coven tends to be a formal affair, with a chain of command and ranks.

The members may be all male, all female, or a mixture of both. Also, a coven can be a training or teaching group with students that learn and others who teach as they all work toward personal advancement and a degree or degrees within their own tradition. For example, you may meet folks from the Cabot, Georgian, Gardnerian, or Alexandrian traditions. (This is just a thumbnail sketch; explaining the dynamics of a coven could fill an entire book on its own.)

A circle, on the other hand, is a much less formal group. The members of a circle may not all practice the same flavor of the Craft (such as Eclectic, Celtic, Norse, Strega, or even a kitchen Witch). They can be a mixed group or all the same gender. Even so, any positive path is welcome in a circle. This way, they can all share information and ideas, and best of all, they learn from each other. In a circle, all of the members are considered equal to one another. How do they pull that off without dissension among the ranks, you may wonder? Well, a circle is about building a magickal family and about the bonds of friendship. Yes, some circle mates may have more experience than other members, but what keeps the group together is a the chance to study, learn, and to grow together in that spirit of friendship.

Now that you have an idea of what a circle is, what points should you keep in mind if you feel you would like the opportunity to work with a group of other Witches? To start, I would recommend that you keep working on your intuition and learning to sense psychic energy. This comes in very handy when you work with a group. Solid magickal development and personal power are also bonuses, which is exactly why we have been working on all those points so far. These traits are important because you have to have your personal power centered before you do group work. It is a very good idea to have a handle on your strengths and weaknesses and to know who you are, magickally speaking, before you jump in the magickal sandbox with all the other kids.

Here is a big secret I'm going to let you in on; consider it one of the "mysteries" of the Craft. Group work is not a crutch for individuals who feel they cannot perform magick on their own. No, indeed. Instead, group work is about being confident in your own magickal personality, style, and talents to the point that you are willing to combine your own skills with others. In turn, this gives you another opportunity for growth and personal advancement, should you wish it.

The endearing elegance of female friendship ...
SAMUEL JOHNSON

MAGICKAL FRIENDS ARE LIKE FAMILY

There is a special sort of psychic energy and vibe to a good circle, which is interesting since Witches tend to be very individual people. The personalities and backgrounds of the members of the circle vary widely; however, there is something about them that makes them all click together. The members of a circle all share the same wavelength, so to speak. Some will be outgoing and others will be more laid-back, yet they all bring something unique to the group, and their energies complement each other. In other words, they may all be singing their own tune, but together it somehow creates a fabulous multi-part harmony.

For example, in my circle, while we may share many things in common, such as herbalism and a love for gardening, we also bring our own unique experiences to the group's energy. A few of us are more soft-spoken and serious, and a few are outgoing and funny. A few members of the group get really enthusiastic and excited at circle get-togethers and have a hard time settling down, and of course there is a person or two who you have to poke just to get them up and moving. Some ladies are casual and go with the flow, and others are more organized and serious.

Out of the ten of us, five are married. A few are happily divorced and living the single life, while another few are living in committed relationships. About half of the group have children. The ages of our children range from just-out-of-the-nest twenties to college-aged kids, high-school age, middle school, elementary, and brand-new babies.

We range in ages from our late forties to our twenties. All live within a forty-five-mile radius of each other. Some members live in the city, while others live across the river in the suburbs or even farther out in the country. Professionally we are also a diverse group. Half of the group have college degrees; a few of us went back to school to take continuing education classes. In this group we have an artist, a physical therapist, a couple of writers, a full-time new mom, and a graduate student who has just received her degree in forestry. Two other women work at different area colleges, one in the student development department of a large technical school and the other in the science department at a community college. We have a paralegal who is also an aromatherapist, a pharmacy technician, and one of the members works at a major university in cancer research and treatment. How's that for variety?

So with this type of group, what do you suppose we could all have in common? Witchcraft and magick. We share a reverence for the natural world and an appreciation for nature. There is a bond of friendship and a sense of respect for each other's experiences and magickal knowledge. We have fun, and we honestly enjoy each other's company. And that is what makes for a successful circle.

START WITH A STUDY GROUP

To start your own circle, keep it simple. I would begin with a few magickal friends. Try setting aside a convenient time, once a month, to get together and to then study together. Pick a topic ahead of time. Take turns hosting the study group, and each of you should take a turn at choosing your subject, which is an opportunity to share with the others what you know best. For example, if one of you is into crystals, they could bring along a few favorite books and personal notes or handouts and share this information with the others. Ironically, one of the best ways to learn more about a personal favorite topic is to offer to teach it. Then you get the chance to consider the information you have and how to present it so that your friends will enjoy learning about it. Or if you don't feel like you are up to that, another good starting idea is to choose a magickal book to discuss.

You should each acquire a copy of the book, and then give each other a month to read and study it. Put together an informal book report, and then when you get together you can discuss it and share notes. This leads to a lively discussion on what you learned, how the information helped you, and, last but not least, whether the spells worked— that type of thing. What is interesting about this is that I have rarely met two people who took away the same information out of a book. Finding out what another person's thoughts are can give you a perspective you hadn't considered before, as well as give you plenty to discuss and to share.

Another option is to take a class together. Sign up for a class at the local magickal shop, or perhaps attend a free gardening lecture at a nursery. Most importantly of all, take your time and get to know each other. You are better off starting out with a core group of two or three friends before you dive into the dynamics of working with a large group of acquaintances. So don't rush things, and see how things develop over time. You are much better off building that friendship and comfort level with each other gradually than tossing a bunch of strangers together and wondering why everyone is stiff and uncomfortable.

Usually, after a few months, someone has a friend who is interested in coming to your study get-togethers, and then you can all meet and see how you get along with the new person. Invite them as a guest and see how you all interact with each other. Some of these new people may wish to stay and continue working with your group, and others may only be curious. So give it time and see what happens. Then later, if everyone agrees, you can invite them to join. Before you know it, someone else has a friend or relative, and then your study group jumps from two or three to five or six.

A friend may well be reckoned
the masterpiece of Nature.
RALPH WALDO EMERSON

THE NEXT STEP IN BUILDING A CIRCLE

Once your study group has been together for a while, you may wish to try a simple ritual together. I know that was the case with my first study group, many years ago. We had all taken the time to get to know each other and to enjoy each other's company. Then it was decided that it was time to test the magickal waters. So we all discussed the idea and then decided who would do what—in this case, call the quarters and cast a circle. I asked who would be comfortable with which elemental quarter, and since there were four of us, it fell into place nicely. Two of us had some group experience and the others had not—so we talked it out and came up with a working plan. We got the kids settled with a few videos, then we trooped off to the hostess's backyard to see what was what.

It was a clear and pleasant summer night. Lots of stars sparkled down from above, and a waxing moon was about halfway up in the sky. However, the moment we stepped outside, every neighbor around started peeking out the windows. While it was embarrassing to be the center of the neighborhood's attention, we were determined to stretch our wings a bit. So there we stood, attired in T-shirts and shorts: Crystal, our hostess, who was blithely ignoring her neighbors; myself; a nervous and shy Nimue; and tough and feisty Brigit, our newest member.

At first, we went to our chosen quarters, stood in a loose circle, and centered ourselves. Then I saw Brigit open her eyes and frown at the neighborhood contingent. I turned around and grimaced at the two male neighbors who were now standing right at the back fence, about ten feet away. They were leaning over the fence and leering.

"Well, hell," Brigit grumbled.

"Oh, they always stare when I come out here at night," Crystal admitted with a shrug.

"Can't we do anything about that? We are Witches." Brigit frowned and then narrowed her eyes in concentration. "Hey, Miss Psychic—can't you fix that?" she challenged me with a conspirator's grin.

We all started to chuckle, I believe a comment was made about toads, and then I had an idea. "Let me try a little something," I murmured to them.

I asked everyone to join hands, and then I squeezed Brigit's hand on my right and quietly asked her to lend me some energy, which she did without hesitation. (I was curious to see what would happen if I added someone else's willing energy.) I reached out with my senses and felt the curiosity of the two men standing at the back fence. Then I tapped into their nervousness of what would happen if their wives happened to catch them staring at their pretty blond neighbor and her friends and turned it to my advantage.

I silently gave the nosey neighbors a little mental push to go back inside and to leave us alone. About twenty seconds later, both neighbors abruptly went inside. All the back porch lights clicked off, and we were left alone. We let go of each other's hands and centered ourselves. (Yes, I know that psychic trick is walking the line. Bad Ellen. No cookie.) I had turned their curiosity against them and influenced those leering neighbors. At the time I believe I justified it by telling myself it was defensive and I was protecting the group.

Actually, looking back all those years ago, I realize that I was just showing off, which today makes me cringe. I never said I was perfect, especially when my temper is involved. It took me some time (years) to realize that just because I could mess with people's heads didn't mean that I should. Why do you suppose I am always so careful to warn others about the consequences of manipulation?

So back to the story. Now that we had a bit of privacy, we decided to begin to quietly call the quarters. I called the east, Nimue called the south, Crystal called the west, and then Brigit stepped up, tossed out her hands, and called the north. I could feel the push of her energy against my chest, and in unison the whole group took a step back, as if choreographed.

Whoa, Brigit definitely packed a punch. We joined hands again and had a chance to experience the energy that flowed around the circle from member to member. Sweat popped out on our brows, and I could feel the energy gather in the solar plexus area. Impressed with each other, we all grinned and then took a few moments and got used to the sensations. After a short time, we released the quarters, grounded the energy, and opened the circle. We sat on the grass talking for a while, and then when the six kids all came outside demanding Popsicles, we adjourned to the house to discuss our discovery and break out the snacks.

While my daughter, Brigit's two kids, and Crystal's young brood ran around making an unholy mess with Popsicles, the ladies sat down at the table, passed around the snacks we had all brought along, and shared what each of our impressions were during the quarter calling and how we each physically experienced our combined energy.

As a group, we had learned something new and had expanded upon the friendship that we were all building with each other. Together we could raise quite a bit of energy, and we started making plans for our next get-together so we could try a full ritual and cast a spell together.

Energy falls just short of being joy.
Mason Cooley

Sensing Energy in a Group Setting: A Psychic Group Exercise

Remember the energy ball exercise from chapter 3? I mentioned that there was a way to practice this with a circle or coven, and here it is. This is a great exercise to work with your circle so you can all get to know each other and your personal energies better. This will help you identify who is a projective personality and who is receptive. Plus it will show you immediately what the group's magickal talents are. First, make sure everyone has a pen and a sheet of paper so they can write down their impressions. Then have everyone in the group sit in a circle.

To begin, have one person build the energy ball and then pass it off and around the circle in a clockwise motion. Have the builder jot down a few keywords about what they envisioned and then tuck the paper out of sight. Clockwise, around the circle, from person to person, the energy ball is silently passed. Each individual should hold it for no more than ten seconds. Sense the energy ball and see what your intuition and instincts tell you. As they pass the energy ball to their neighbor, each person should quickly jot down what information they picked up, also putting the paper out of sight. Remember to keep the ball moving so the energy ball doesn't fade.

After the energy ball works its way back around the circle, it is handed back to the builder. The builder should ground the energy ball back into the earth by turning their hands over and pressing their hands to the floor. Wait a moment, make sure everyone has their impressions written down, then have the builder tell the group what the energy ball was. Take turns going around the circle, comparing notes, and see how everyone did. I bet you'll be surprised at the results.

When my circle did this for the first time, I was the builder. I built an energy ball full of swirling, green, heart-shaped ivy leaves. I imagined them tumbling over and over inside the energy ball. When we were done and the group compared notes, we all were quite amazed. Some of the circle's impressions included green swirls, fluttering pink and loving hearts, falling autumn leaves, green leafy herbs, and finally butterflies.

All in all, the images made sense. Some people picked up on the color, which was green. Some correctly interpreted that it was a plant. Others felt the shapes (the heart) or sensed the movement (the swirling autumn leaves, the fluttering hearts, and the butterflies). A few picked up on my emotions and did not get any visual images at all. It all comes down to the magickal individual and how they will perceive and intuit the psychic information.

Continue the exercise and allow everyone a chance to be the builder. Yes, you will find that some folks may be spot-on when it comes to sensing whatever the energy ball is, and others will be better at loading the images into the energy ball for others to sense. And that's to be expected. Some folks are better at projecting psychic images, and others are better at sensing or receiving those images.

VISIONARIES, EMPATHS, AND INTUITIVES, OH MY!

Once you have finished, take a break and make sure that everyone grounds and centers. Compare your notes, and look at them carefully. The best part of this exercise is that it shows you how your circle mates distinguish or perceive psychic and magickal energy. Want a sure-fire way to find out what sort of magickal strengths are in your group? Then here's your big chance.

So, did they see, intuit, or feel their answers in the energy ball exercise? Take a good look at their written responses. If they have described visual images most often, then they are visionary individuals. They are receiving the impressions from their third eye. These visionary types bring a sense of coordination to your circle. They can help plan and will be the ones who create the most visually pleasing altar setup. Visionaries like things to look attractive and balanced. They will be able to envision the magick that your circle performs. They are probably talented at seeing auras and magickal energy, and they are excellent at plotting out rituals, spells, and magick, since they can perfectly picture the positive changes that they are working toward.

Now, if they usually describe feelings and emotions in their notes, then they are more empathic. They are pulling in the information through their solar plexus, and their own emotions and those of the other circle members are also clueing them in. These folks are important additions to a circle's group energy, since they are often concerned about how everyone is feeling. Is the group mood a happy one? Does everyone feel physically comfortable and at ease? If someone is emotionally upset, then the empaths of your group will be the first ones to offer a supportive hand to hold or to give a pat on the back or the all-important hug. These perceptive souls will be ultra-sensitive to the mood and tone of your rituals and magick, more so than the others. They will keep your group compassionate, friendly, kind, and loving.

Finally, if they "just know" and are often extremely accurate—as in word-for-word with what the builder wrote down—then they are using their intuition. This power comes from the crown chakra, and you will often hear them make comments like, "I just knew..."or "It just popped into my head." These intuitive folks are going to be insightful additions to your group. They will be the ones who keep communication and creativity flowing. They will help keep your circle organized and on track. The intuitive practitioner will make good decisions and will know right away without any fuss when the group's energy is on track and when your magick has accomplished its goal. They are very practical and insightful people—so pay attention to them and see what you can learn together as a group.

If You Want to Build a Successful Circle, Then Get Organized

Beltane day three years ago turned out quite differently than my circle had planned. Over the years, the study group had slowly expanded out to a solid working group of eight. Some members had left, and new people had joined, with two more women expressing an interest in joining, which brought us up to ten members. The circle meetings usually ended up at my house, since I had the largest and most private outdoor space. But I was getting tired of trying to get my teenagers to clear out for the evening, not to mention the cleaning beforehand and trying to keep the noise of up to ten women and their kids—who were all talking and laughing—down to a dull roar. Since my husband worked nights and was usually taking a nap before he went to work, this was a dicey prospect at best. Grumbling was ensuing at my house, my kids were complaining, and so was my husband. I was between the old rock and a hard place.

A few days before Beltane, I sat down with my circle mates and friends Nimue and Morgan and told them that something had to give. The family was annoyed, and I was tired of everyone getting together and looking at me to write and design the rituals. After writing all day, I didn't want to be writing rituals for the group each and every time too. I wanted to relax and enjoy myself. Besides, we spent more time gabbing than we did focused on magick, and I knew I wasn't the only one who wanted a change.

Nimue promised to help the group become more structured and organized, and hinted at a circle project that she had in the works. Morgan agreed to take on a more active leadership role within the group. I was happy that we were all thinking along the same lines and was ready step back and let someone else direct the evenings. So with relief, I looked forward to our next get-together, and Nimue, Morgan, and I figured out we would bring up the subject and try to get the ladies more organized starting on Beltane.

Beltane day dawned, and with it, plans to go to Brigit's house for the celebration. Brigit had made her ritual plans and was ready to go. What she didn't count on was having complications from a tooth extraction and an allergic reaction to a prescription. She called me in a panic that afternoon and explained her trip to the emergency room. Now that she had a new prescription, she was really loopy and out of it, not to mention swollen. She could barely talk. She couldn't find the other ladies' phone numbers. Could I make a few calls and let everyone know? I urged her to go to bed and to take care of herself. Promising to send her some healing energy, we rang off.

With only a few hours until everyone arrived at my house so we could carpool together, I started making phone calls. I called Mary first. I caught her while she was gardening and as we talked, I could hear her toddler son racing around the backyard.

"Change of plans," I sighed and filled her in on what had been happening. I was totally frustrated. Would we ever get this group organized?

"May I make a suggestion?" Mary paused for a moment and then said, "Why don't we get ourselves more organized starting tonight, and have a strictly business meeting?"

Now she had my attention. "What do you have in mind?" I asked. My mind reeled at the thought of a circle of Witches having a business meeting. "Do we have to wear suits and ties?" I teased her.

"Have everyone meet at your house as planned, only tell them to bring their appointment books and calendars, and we'll plan out the rest of the year—in advance," Mary wisely suggested.

Done. I made a few more phone calls. Ravyn had finals to cram for; Amber and Fiona, our two prospective members, lived the farthest out and also decided to stay home for the evening. Gillian was called into work at the last minute and couldn't attend. I promised to call them the very next day and let them know what we decided about reorganization. I reached the other women, who each pounced on the idea, and Nimue announced mysteriously that she had something for us to see.

That evening, five of us sat around my kitchen table—Morgan, Nimue, Mary, Freya, and myself—each with our appointment books and calendars spread out in front of us, quietly making plans, taking notes, sorting out things, and having a business meeting. Mary, our professional, kept us on track. If she can run the research center of a major university, you know she could whip us into shape.

It was decided to take turns hosting the circles. Whoever was hostess would decide the theme and run the ritual for the evening, with a different circle member teaching a topic or giving a lecture. Generic ritual outlines were printed out and passed around. A contact sheet or "phone tree" was put together. As for potential lecture topics, Freya, our Norse Witch, offered to teach us more about the runes. Morgan volunteered to do a class on Reiki. Nimue proposed to lecture on the topic of faeries. Mary, also a Master Gardener, offered to teach the ladies about perennial and herb gardening. I suggested a lecture on the Major Arcana of the tarot, and on it went. Mary's enthusiasm was contagious. Ideas were flying fast and furious around the table. Morgan lightly kicked me under the table and we shared a grin. There was hope for this circle yet!

Then our normally quiet Nimue pulled a large stack of file folders out of her bag and handed out some gorgeous, professional-looking folders that she had started. They were filled with notes, color illustrations, and rituals that she had collected from the group over the years, and she had made copies for everyone. She suggested that these would be great for our newest ladies to study and for all of us to have. She'd been working on this project for months. Then she pulled her last surprise out.

"I started an Internet group for us," she shyly announced. "Here is the web address, and I've taken our emails and set us all up as members." We all simply stared. Never underestimate those quiet ones. Nimue had blown us away again with an unexpected insight—or, in this case, a very clever idea. She's sneaky that way.

She smiled and told us that if we wanted, we could go look at the egroup's homepage now. So we all got up, gathered around my computer, and checked out the web page. Nimue explained that now we could post messages to the site and they would automatically go out to the whole group. She showed us the address book she started, a page for photos, a calendar for events, and ritual notes. How cool was that? While we all stood there checking out what she had done, Nimue said with a mischievous grin and nudge to Morgan that what we *really* needed was a logo. As we all went back to the kitchen, I was impressed with what we had so far.

"I feel so official, " I teased them and gestured to the notes, calendars, folders, Internet stuff, and phone lists spread before us.

"Order is always better than chaos," Freya spoke up in a solemn tone with a totally unserious grin as she made notes on a legal pad about the proposed lectures and dates for the year's circle gatherings.

"So speaks the paralegal," Mary chuckled at us all.

In retrospect, Beltane day was not quite the ritual we had all looked forward to; however, we had accomplished quite a bit. Morgan, our artist, agreed to design a logo for the group, which we later posted on our group's web page. Then she went one better and made copies of the artwork that we could slip into the front of a three-ring binder. The binders we all filled with notes and the pretty file folders that Nimue made for us. Morgan also set up a private page to order T-shirts, coffee mugs, and even mouse pads with the group's logo on them, thinking that it would be fun to all wear our circle T-shirts to the next festival we attended as a group.

The circle was in business, and everyone enjoyed the difference that preparing in advance and organization had made for our get-togethers. We all took turns planning and leading rituals and now shared in the responsibilities. The difference it made was simply amazing.

DEDICATING THE GROUP

Here is a lovely idea that was first suggested by the ladies in my circle: a ritual to dedicate the group. This will commemorate an officially chosen group name as it also celebrates your unity and the individual strengths and magick that you each bring to the circle. For this, you will all need to sit down and decide what the circle's name will be. You will also each need to think ahead and decide what specialties you will contribute to your group's knowledge and character. Do you have a knowledge of herbs, crystals, or tarot? Perhaps you contribute art, sewing talents, a skill in Reiki, or you are an adept at runes. On the other hand, maybe you bring to the circle organization skills—which is a talent that would benefit any group.

Setup and Supplies

The setup for this group dedication is uncomplicated but can turn out to be very attractive when everyone contributes a little something to the altar. For this I would use a central small table that you can place in the middle of your working circle. One of those circular decorative end tables works out well—you know, the ones that are about 30 inches across, made of wood, with three support legs, and are extremely plain and then covered with a tablecloth? Set that in the center of your working space and add a new, large white pillar candle to represent the group. Carve a sun and the group's name on the side of the candle, and then place it in its holder. This candle is important to the ceremony and will be used for illumination. Also, you will need as many plain white tealights as you have members. Add a lighter to the table, so you can light the main pillar.

Everyone should bring a small symbol or item that can be used as a physical representation of the knowledge or skill that they are contributing to the circle. Then one by one, during the dedication, they will place their items on the center table, with a simple explanation of what it symbolizes. For example, if you bring organization to the group, try setting out a few pens and papers. If your specialty is the runes, then place a few runes on the altar. Perhaps you are knowledgeable about herbalism and plants; then you could place a small green potted plant or a bag of dried herbs on the altar. Or if you feel that you don't have a specialty just yet, but that you bring enthusiasm and a willingness to learn, perhaps you could place your magickal notebook or even a photo of yourself. Use your imagination, and see what you come up with. I wish you much success and magick as your group grows together.

Ritual Outline

1. Set up the central table. Cover with a cloth, and place the large white pillar candle in a holder in the middle of the table. Arrange the unlit tealights all around the central pillar. (Keep them in easy reach.)

2. Have the members of the group bring their items and gather together in a loose circle around the central table.

3. Light the engraved pillar candle. Ground and center.

4. Call the quarters and cast a circle, as is your group's preference.

5. One by one, going around the circle in a clockwise motion, place your items on the central table with a simple explanation of what each one represents. Say something like this: "I bring to this circle the knowledge of herbs (or runes, Reiki, etc.). I am happy to share this with my circle mates." Or try "I bring enthusiasm and a willingness to learn. I am happy to share my energy with my circle mates."

6. Once all the items have been placed upon the central table, then formally announce the chosen name for the group.

7. Pass the tealights around to each circle member. One at a time, light the individual candles from the large central pillar. As each person lights their individual candle from the pillar candle, they will say, "May the magick of our circle burn brightly within me."

8. Once everyone has their tealight burning, repeat the following spell verse together: "Though the candle flames are many, they symbolize the one.

May our bond of friendship grow and shine bright like the sun. With many voices together, we create a magickal harmony. We dedicate this group, now known as _____. And as we will it, so must it be!"

9. Finally, have everyone carefully set their tealights in a circle once again, about three inches away from and all around the pillar candle (just like they were arranged in the beginning). Make sure that you keep the other objects on the table safely away from the candle flames, as those tealights get hot. If necessary, move the personal items out of the way and arrange them on the floor around the table; better safe than sorry. Allow the tealights to burn until they go out on their own; keep an eye on them as you immediately proceed to step 10.

10. Release the quarters and open the circle. Snuff out the pillar and save for the next group ritual.

11. Break out the snacks.

12. Relax, and enjoy each other's company.

13. Clean up.

Ever the Circle Continues . . .

I hope that these techniques will help you and your magickal group, be it coven or circle, grow in fellowship together. Group work brings its own challenges, but it also brings many joys. There is nothing like standing hand in hand with a close set of Witches and magick users, all working mutually in a spirit of trust and camaraderie. Those bonds of friendship will only grow stronger with time. You will be there to support each other in the tough days and to celebrate the good ones.

I have also noticed that when a circle works together on similar goals, things will begin to fall neatly into place within their own lives. Group magick is powerful, and it creates a sort of ripple effect. When a circle of Witches works magick together for positive purposes such as protection, job security, healing for a friend or relative, to create prosperity, or to bring opportunities and growth, their magick radiates out, not only touching the immediate environment and the folks who are standing in the circle, but flowing out further, into the house or garden where the ritual was performed. That positive force is unstoppable, and it will smoothly roll into the neighborhood and surrounding area, and then beyond even that.

Quality group magick changes everything it touches in subtle ways, and it forever transforms the group who originally cast the magick. As a group, they will then reap those benefits together. I have experienced it in my own circle and seen the magick at work within my own life and my circle mates' lives. If you perform group magick with heart and compassion, you will see the benefits in your daily life as well, which is why we say, "In perfect love and perfect trust, ever the circle continues."

Chapter 6

The goal of life is living

in agreement with nature.

ZENO

Practical Magick:
Living the Life of a Natural Witch

Being a Witch encompasses all aspects of your life, not just the spellcasting parts. After I wrote *Cottage Witchery: Natural Magick for Hearth and Home*, I was surprised by the questions that I received. Folks were curious as to what they should do next after working all the various spells for prosperity, protection, and harmony in the home. They wanted more—which left me trying to explain that the next step was to *live* the magick. The spells are simply the first of many steps. In other words, it's not enough just to bless your home; living as a Witch is also about working and thriving within a blessed house, and this includes your whole environment.

Your environment includes what part of the world you live in, how you live, who lives with you, and in what variety of neighborhood you reside. Is there the hustle and bustle of the city to consider, the structure and tempo of the suburbs, or the relaxed energy of the country? All of these different considerations affect the magickal energy that is present within your world. Taking a moment to reflect on how you as a magickal individual react to and work with all these aspects is key.

So how do you gain the most from your surroundings? I suggest that you begin by tapping into the magick that is inherent in every environment. I will admit there will be days when this is going to seem like a tough order to fill, but use your imagination and follow those instincts that we've been working so hard on developing. Stretch out your feelings, and see what you can discover. What do you suppose would happen if you took a few moments, tuned out all the silly distractions in your life, and really sensed what sort of natural energies and magick was going on all around you? Why, you'd learn to tap into the rhythms of the natural magick that is already there. You would learn to work in harmony with these forces instead of battling against them, no matter where you live.

As a Witch, do you acknowledge the tempo and current of the magick as it swirls around you and your loved ones in your everyday lives? Do you work with your environment and recognize the unique tempo of nature's energy in your own surroundings? No matter where you live—in the city, suburbs, or in the country—magick is there. Sure, it may be easier to feel that connection to the earth while standing on the beach and watching the moon or the sun rise over the ocean or even watching it set below the tree line in the woods. But most of us live in urban or suburban areas, and we face more of a challenge maintaining that connection to nature, her seasons, and the psychic energies of the Wheel of the Year.

A few years ago, I was fortunate to be able to travel to Chicago for a book signing. Maybe it makes me sound like a rube, but I had never stayed in such a large city before. As my husband and I drove next to the shore of Lake Michigan along the edge of the city, I was amazed by just how big Chicago really is. (Yeah, yeah, go ahead and snicker.) Chicago impressed me. We arrived on a cloudy day, and you couldn't even see the tops of many of the skyscrapers, which gave it a very otherworldly feel. After checking in to our hotel, my husband and I hit the pavement and walked around the city. There was a very different type of rhythm there. At first it seemed alien to me, as there were no trees in this part of downtown but there was lots of traffic, noise, and people. We grabbed a quick bite in a café and sat at the window to people-watch. The energy and tempo of the city was contagious, and even my husband commented on the different "vibe" that was in the air.

I recall sitting there and wondering how in the world folks who live deep in the concrete jungles felt and kept their connection to the earth and to their nature religion. Maybe they had to dig a little deeper, or perhaps they were just more clever at it. Then again, I imagine the folks who thrive in the city wonder how in the world people can stand living in the suburbs. There is a unique magickal energy to every city and to each environment; the trick is to pull it in and use it to your advantage.

There is a way to use that perception that we've been developing and to intuitively change the magick to suit your own surroundings. It requires you to step outside of the box, use your imagination, and stretch out your psychic senses and intuition.

Magick is in every environment.

Christopher Penczak

Enchanting Your Environment

Some of the best things about a city are its history and its architecture. The different ethnic districts within a large city all have their own culture and history. While each of these will have its own magickal type of atmosphere, the important thing for a city dweller is to tune in and to work in harmony with each different environment. Even while in the midst of the city, you can find the four elements. Fire is represented by the sunlight or even by the illumination of the skyline at night. Air is pretty self-explanatory: the sky or the breeze as it blows by. Water is represented by rain or snow. For earth, if there are no trees around, in a pinch you can always work with the concrete beneath your feet. (While my gardener's soul whimpers at the thought of no soil to play in, my husband pointed out to me that concrete is made of crushed stone.)

Hmm, well, you could also argue that the stone used in the buildings could represent the earth too. And what about the metal beams and frames of the skyscrapers? I don't see why that wouldn't work, as metal is one of the five magickal Chinese elements. Anyway, use your imagination! Tap into the rhythm of the people all around you. There is a powerhouse of energy there.

I have heard folks refer to the modern big cities as being similar to the forest primeval. Well, I can see that. The inner city can be a wild place, and it can certainly be a dangerous one, too, if you are unaware or careless. However, there is more diversity in the cities, hence there are more cultural opportunities as well. Attend a symphony, concert, or play. Enjoy a street festival, and try different ethnic foods. Experience all the wonders and the cultures that are available to you. Also don't forget to take advantage of the formal parks, public gardens, zoos, and botanical gardens. Use this as an excuse to snoop around your city and check out a few museums and parks—see what you can find!

Also, don't forget that older homes within your city have gardens and balconies that will be turned into tiny oases, and lush miniature courtyards and pocket gardens will pop up here and there. When you stumble across these small green spaces in the city, acknowledge them for the magick they bring. If no green space is available to you, then bring the natural energy of plants into your homes. Try growing some easy-to-care-for houseplants, and bring a touch of nature inside with you.

I can bear a charmed life.

SHAKESPEARE

SUBURBAN SORCERESS AND COUNTRY CHARM

Living in the 'burbs has its own set of challenges. Sure, you can plant up your yard to your little heart's content, but unless you have a large yard or a privacy fence, you may be in the middle of a goldfish bowl the moment you step outside. I have a sibling who lives in a large, beautiful home in a very expensive neighborhood. They have a gorgeous deck and landscaped yard—and absolutely no privacy. You step out the back door, and everyone from six houses around can see you. When I suggested they plant some trees or a hedge to give them privacy, they were shocked and pointed out that half the point was in being seen.

Umm, okay. Suddenly my little fifty-year-old ranch-style house, which is in the city limits if I want to get technical, seemed much more appealing. So I don't have five bathrooms or three stories overlooking the neighbor's hot tub, but I do have an older neighborhood with diversity and character. We live right outside the historic district, close to a university, and there are large elm, oak, and maple trees in my yard, plus all the other neighborhood trees—not to mention the blooming dogwoods, crab apples, and magnolias in the vicinity. Kids ride their bikes, parents walk their babies in strollers, older kids skateboard, and in the fall we are serenaded by the marching band and the sounds of football games from the nearby high school. We like our older neighborhood.

So while I think of myself as living in the 'burbs, I imagine there are others who would consider me to live in the city, too. How about that? Could I be between the worlds? I don't see why not. I planted up my suburban Witch's gardens and saved up to put in a privacy fence to create a secret garden area. I planted assorted blooming shrubs along the fence rows to create a modern sort of hedgerow and to give us more privacy. I live and practice my craft quite nicely here in the suburbs, in a modern and very natural Witch kind of way. Essentially, I tap into the nature and the energy of the seasons that is around me, and I put it to excellent use.

If you live in the country or a rural area and have private open spaces or secluded wooded areas, well, good for you! Acknowledge your blessing of the surrounding natural areas, and take your time getting to know the character of the land. While you have the gift of privacy, you may feel a bit isolated and cut off from the rest of your brothers and sisters in the Craft. But just remember, when you are out there under the light of the full moon, standing alone in the wild places as did the earliest Witches, that you are never truly alone.

Because all of us, as magickal practitioners, Witches, Wiccans, and Pagans, share a psychic and spiritual connection to each other. On those evenings when you are working under the full moon, know that even as you stand alone in your backyard gardens or living rooms, your brothers and sisters in the Craft from all over the world are out there standing with you. If you stretch out your intuition, you will feel their strength and the magickal bond that links us all together. If you like, here is a spell that you can cast no matter where you live that will help you feel and rejoice in that sense of fellowship and connection.

RITUAL OF CONNECTION

For this ritual, the supply list is short and sweet: you will need a white jar candle (something that is safe to burn for several hours), yourself, and a full moon night. Light the jar candle and move to a place where you have a view of the full moon as it rises. If possible, I would perform this outside under that full moon, but in a pinch it will also work indoors.

Visualize a fine silver type of cord that connects your solar plexus to nature and to the other Witches, Wiccans, and Pagans that are scattered all over the world. Next, visualize that they in turn are also connected in a spirit of friendship to you. Out and out the web spins, and more and more shimmering strands are added and spun. Focus on this magickal web and the feeling of a gentle and positive spiritual connection.

Think about the phrase "In perfect love and perfect trust." This is a positive use of your personal power; it's not about linking into someone who is unwilling. There are many open and friendly magickal individuals out there; consider this exercise a bit of an astral handshake. If you notice that your solar plexus area tightens a bit, that's fine, just keep going. After a short time, you will feel a bit warmer, and your link will feel more defined. At this point, repeat the spell verse:

> *I am connected to others by shimmering strands,*
>
> *Under the moon so bright, together as one we stand.*
>
> *In the ways of magick, I sense many others with me,*
>
> *Weaving our magick together in loving harmony.*
>
> *Bringing harm to none, and with a sprinkle of moon dust,*
>
> *I release this web, in perfect love and perfect trust.*

Now take a deep breath and look up at the moon. In your own words, ask for the blessings and ancient wisdom of the full moon to shine gently into your life and into your home environment. Then allow the strand at your solar plexus to unravel. See in your mind's eye that the web begins to loosen and to disintegrate on its own, in accordance with the free will of all and for the good of all. Ground and center when you are finished. Move the candle to a safe, fireproof spot where it can continue to burn until it goes out on its own.

> *When humor goes, there goes civilization.*
>
> Erma Bombeck

How to Deal with Nonmagickal Spouses, In-laws, and Parents

Now that we've taken the time to consider our environments and how they affect our magick and our lives, we should also consider how the other people in our lives affect us as well. We all have friends, relatives, and loved ones that are part of our lives, and—like it or not—they do affect you, your environment, and your magick, especially if you are in the broom closet to avoid problems, or even if the people in your life know about your craft.

In my experience, families tend to react in a number of ways to the fact that one of their loved ones is a Witch. Over the years, I have seen them all. And after a while, I stopped taking it personally, and my sense of humor took over (much to my relatives' dismay)! Now, if you find this information offensive or too sarcastic—sorry. But I think sometimes the best thing you can do is to look at things from a new perspective, laugh out loud about the situations life throws your way, and to go on. After all, you can't choose your relatives—but you definitely can have a little fun while you deal with them. Remember, we want to work *with* your environment, not battle against it. So take a deep breath, unclench a bit, and prepare to cackle.

The Various Scenarios You Are Likely to Encounter

We start out with the "concerned" relatives—and you'll know they are concerned because they always start out the conversation with, "Please don't be mad, but I'm very *concerned* . . ." These folks can either go overboard and try to have an intervention, or they get upset when you don't immediately fall into line and may not speak to you for a while, thus employing an oldie but goodie: the "cold shoulder" form of punishment. The cold shoulder is still an effective tool for families to try and bring around a "difficult" relative. Occasionally they may really get inventive, sending you pamphlets in the mail or trying to read you Bible verses, or they'll whip out the "fear and guilt" card, which is played with the declaration that they are worried about your soul and are so sad that they ultimately won't be seeing you in heaven.

To this, my response was, "Look, I can't stand being around you now at family functions. What makes you think we'd be hanging around together in the afterlife?" This response was delivered in the most pleasant tone, with a friendly pat on the shoulder and a smile. I think the relative in question is still trying to figure out if I was joking or serious.

Then there is the teary-eyed approach. They are distraught, after all—and they want to make damn sure that you know *they* are the ones who are suffering. The distressed family member will look at you with tear-filled eyes and announce in a shaking voice that "I'll pray for you"—as if you are headed off to a horrible fate or something—to which my response is to say with a big smile, as if they've given me a compliment, "Well, thanks! I'll pray for you, too!" They never know how to react to that one.

Sometimes families do the pink elephant routine. What, you aren't familiar with that one? Oooh, I'll be happy to share it with you—and I'll bet you that you have already dealt with it. You just may have been blissfully unaware that it had a name. This routine goes like this: the family will treat your Witchcraft as if it were a big pink elephant that sits in the corner, with the absolute conviction that if they just ignore the pink elephant, then it doesn't exist. If they don't look at the pink elephant or talk about the pink elephant, then maybe, just maybe, it will all go away. It's also known as denial—and no, *denial* is not just a river in Egypt.

There is also the "Wow, that is so cool—I can't wait to tell all my friends" scenario. I know one Witch who was informed by her mother that dear old mom had told all the ladies at the local country club that her daughter was a Witch. When the Witch in question—who up until then had been keeping a very low profile—sputtered in disbelief at her mother, she was blithely informed, "Well, dear, it *was* the week before Halloween. And really, the country club ladies were just *fascinated.*"

Then there is the Oh-my-god-what-if-someone-finds-out (or the Darren Stephens Syndrome, which is straight from the old television show *Bewitched*). Come on, you remember: Darren was always fussing at Samantha for using her magick—*until* he needed something, and then, well, *that* was okay. With this routine, the family member is convinced that their own personal lives or reputations will go straight to hell because they are related to a Witch. And it goes a little something like this …

So okay honey, you can do your thing, just please keep it a secret. Keep your witchy friends away from the house and make sure you don't wear any magickal jewelry in public or do anything that could ever make anyone suspect that you might not be—well, just like everyone else.

"But … there's just one thing, and I really hate to ask," says the family member in a conspirator's whisper, "I was wondering, do you think you could work a spell to help me get over the flu/get that raise/sell my house quickly/nab some overtime?" They make the request with a nervous smile and then finish it up with, "Really, I know you are into this stuff and it's no big deal. This will just be our little secret."

Does any of this sound familiar to you? Yeah, I thought so. So how do you deal with this? You dig down and find a sense of humor. It's tough, and it is a challenge that all of us face from time to time, but you will rise to the occasion and climb above the difficulties. Now that we've had a good chuckle, here is yet another practical issue that can affect your magickal life. And this time, you will need all the wisdom, magickal expertise, and humor that you can possibly muster.

Mother Nature is providential.
She gives us twelve years to develop
a love for our children before
turning them into teenagers.

WILLIAM GALVIN

WITCH PARENTS AND THEIR TEENS: ARE WE HAVING FUN YET?

For those readers who imagine my life to be a faerie tale where everyone gets along and no family arguments about the Craft ever happen … oh boy, are you in for a rude awakening. Hello, this is real life. My family has dealt with the ups and downs of day-to-day life as well as the challenges and joys of the Craft. For those of you who are also doing the best you can with your kids, I thought I would share some of my experiences so you can see that no, you are not alone, and that we all have situations and challenges to deal with.

When the kids are small, it's not so bad—they enjoy the magickal holidays, and they enjoy learning about nature from a different spiritual perspective. I mean, how many other kids' parents teach them about the lady of the moon or the faeries? But when they become teenagers, then suddenly everyone else's opinion is more important than their parents'.

You become uncool overnight, and somehow you've also become incredibly stupid in their eyes, which just sucks all around. After all, they already know everything, you don't have to tell them. Also, they want you to be involved with them—just not *too* involved. They want you to attend all their school functions—just please don't embarrass them— and to that I wish you good luck. Teens are like chameleons. Their mood changes so fast you can only try and keep up. If you want drama, tragedy, and triumph in your daily life, then all you need is a teenager.

Now my brood has grown up with a mother who worked the psychic fairs and who has quietly practiced the Craft all their lives. As we live in the Midwest, I kept a fairly low profile and just went about my business. While all of my kids were taught the Craft basics, I never forced the issue. Their choice of spirituality has always been up to them. It wasn't until my first book, *Garden Witchery*, was published that things got interesting, as this took me out of the shadows and pretty much out of the broom closet. At the time, all three of my kids were in high school; my oldest was finishing up his senior year, my second son was a junior, and my daughter was a freshman.

The oldest hated high school, thought it was lame, and couldn't wait to graduate. He honestly didn't care if people found out. His opinion was that it was nobody's business, and he was proud and excited for me, as he knew how hard I had worked to make this dream a reality.

The youngest was at the time dressing in a trendy sort of gothic theme, loved the Craft, and was making excellent grades. She was in track, a member of the marching band, and in her "Witchcraft yeah!" mode. She took an active part in my circle's gatherings and was proud to consider herself a Witch.

On the opposite end of the spectrum, the middle son was a starter on the varsity football team and in the honors program. He was a bit concerned what would happen if his teammates or friends at school found out. He hoped that he wouldn't have to deal with any fallout, and he never did. I honestly don't believe anyone else really cared.

Even when I was interviewed on the morning news, most of the comments were along the lines of "Hey, was that your mom on the news? She wrote a book about gardens or something? That's cool." Most folks weren't clueing in, and so on our life went. Things stayed pretty much the same; there were no confrontations, and if a friend or two of the kids found out about the books, they were usually pretty excited. So for a few years, things flowed along and our family life wasn't affected too much.

Well, honestly, I'm a very practical Witch and a regular gal. It's not like I stand out in the front yard in flowing black robes, waving a banner at every passing car that proclaims my religious beliefs. Oh, please. If I'm out in the yard, I'm probably gardening. When I teach classes, lecture, or do an author event, I am in street clothes: a nice outfit, a flattering pantsuit, or a dress. It's chancy enough toting around books, a briefcase, and such while being all dressed up and in high heels. The last thing I want to do is deal with long, dramatic sleeves or a floor-length dress. Besides, I don't have anything to prove.

The years went by, and the boys graduated and began working part time while attending community college on scholarships. And then our youngest, our daughter, became a high-school senior. That's when things got dicey. Gone was the gothic look. This girl had one goal and one goal only: to attend a four-year university. She waitressed on the weekends, tucking away money into her savings like crazy, all with the dream of saving up toward tuition. She wanted a degree in history and archeology. She'd apply for scholarships, grants, and take out loans, but she was determined to go away to school to a university. We all backed her up one hundred percent. If this was her dream, we'd help her find a way.

Somewhere during the beginning of her senior year, she went from "Witchcraft yeah!" to "Oh-my-god-I-don't-want-anybody-to-know-that-my-mom-is-a-Witch"—which I will admit was damn near impossible. I had several books published now. I taught classes on the Craft locally, and even the major chain bookstore in town had hosted a few book signings. Now, whenever we walked in there to shop, I was greeted by name by the managers and employees and asked what new book I was working on. Occasionally they would ask what I thought of the New Age section or the seasonal Witchcraft-themed endcap displays. This *so* wasn't a secret anymore.

Since my daughter is also an avid reader, she was usually with me at the bookstore, and she would bristle and stalk away every time, muttering "I'm going to be in the history section." And I began to notice that my daughter was flip-flopping back and forth about how she felt about her mom becoming more well known as a writer and how she felt about me being a public Witch. One day it was exciting, the next day she brooded about it and told me it was annoying.

For example, the day she went to have her senior pictures taken, she asked me to come along. And as it turned out, one of the people who worked at the studio recognized me and commented on how much they enjoyed my books. My daughter frowned at me and slipped into a dressing room to change her outfit, which gave me a moment to chat and to thank the person, and then to remind them gently that this was my daughter's day, so I wanted to keep the focus on her.

I mentally held my breath, figuring that my daughter would be angry that I had been recognized in public. But no, she seemed to shrug this one off. As we drove home, she asked me about it, so I answered her. Her response was that it was very cool that Witches were found everywhere—there's that chameleon quality again; maybe things weren't so bad.

Until she came home one afternoon in October of her senior year in an incredibly poor mood because a friend (who was also a cute guy) had taken her aside in concern about a rumor that he had heard. Silly me. I thought she was stressed out about the play tryouts that were coming up.

Yeah, you guessed it. The rumor was, "Isn't your mom a Witch? They say she writes books on it and everything."

To which my daughter's answer was to say no, and to lie and say that she didn't have any idea what he was talking about.

Now I had a problem on my hands. She could have just laughed this off or said nothing, if she was uncomfortable with his question. Jeez, she'd been handling other questions like this with style for years. She had even helped me coach her older brothers on good or humorous responses for them to use.

I was flabbergasted and couldn't believe that she lied about it. I asked her what story she was going to invent the next time someone handed her a book with my picture inside of it and said, "Hey, that's your mom!" (Because that had happened already the summer before.)

I mean, honestly, was she going to come up with a "No, that's just my mother's evil twin" story? After an hour of top-volume arguing, capped off with her tearfully yelling that I just didn't understand, our happy home wasn't very happy.

Actually I did and do understand. Being a teenager is incredibly hard. They want to be an individual, but they are also afraid to stand out too much. At this point in their lives, they are deciding who and what they want to be. It's a tough time for any teen. And having a mother who writes books about Witchcraft takes it into a whole new league.

After things calmed down a bit, I asked her if she still considered herself a Witch, and she tearfully nodded her head yes. She just preferred to practice privately and as a solitary. Well, I certainly had no problems with that. However, I suggested to her that she needed to quit going back and forth with her feelings about the Craft, because she didn't get to have it both ways. I also cautioned her to carefully think about her actions that day, since when a Witch lies, it lessens the power of their spoken words. And no, that didn't go over very well either. She stomped off to her room and slammed the door.

A bit later, I heard her stereo kick up and could smell patchouli candles and some dragon's-blood incense burning in her room—the combination she typically uses to combat negativity and bad vibes. I didn't know whether to be offended or proud that she had thought to use it. I went for proud.

For the next few days, things were strained at home. My husband and I also argued about the situation, and my sons decided to voice their opinion and told their sister to get over it already—and was that a pleasant afternoon. Eventually everything cooled down. Then my daughter informed me that she was heading out to the public library to get a copy of the finally announced school play. Tryouts were at the end of the week.

That evening she quietly approached me and asked if I would run some lines with her, as she wanted to practice for her audition. Relieved that she was speaking to me again and didn't seem to be angry anymore, I popped up enthusiastically and didn't even think to look at the title of the play. She handed me the book, and I asked her what page to turn to. Then I saw the title.

The play was *The Crucible*.

No, I am not making this stuff up. These are the type of family situations I deal with. Personally, I think my sense of humor helps to keep me sane. At least my life isn't boring . . .

Well, now the mystery was solved as to why all the Witch rumors were swirling around high school. It was close to Halloween, and the high-school play was about the freaking Salem Witch trials! Goddess, give me strength. My gaze shot up to hers, and I bit my tongue to hold back my anger. My daughter looked defensive and nervous.

I tried for a nonconfrontational tone and failed, beautifully. "Are you kidding me?" I asked her incredulously.

She launched into a speech about how this was an important part of American history and that she wanted to audition for Abigail, the main character who was the manipulative, cruel ringleader of the accusing girls. I sat back on the couch, groaned, and put my head in my hands.

Honestly, I didn't know whether to laugh or to cry. "After everything that's happened in the last few weeks, you don't expect me to approve of this, do you?" I asked her.

"It's just a play, Mom," she argued and then proceeded to tell me that the play made the accusers look incredibly bad—that the focus was on how one horrible girl ruined so many lives, all because she got dumped by a married man.

"And this is the character you want to portray?" I sputtered.

She started another impassioned debate of the pros of her being in this play. I could only think of the cons. Well, ultimately this had to be her decision—not mine. I sincerely hoped she wouldn't regret it.

I fell back on my standard operating procedure when things get tense: humor. "Aw, sis," I sighed in resignation, "they'll toss me out of the union for this."

"What union?" she questioned.

"The Witches' Union," I shot back with a grin. She rolled her eyes at me for being a smart-ass and asked for my help with practicing for her audition again. So I helped her practice her lines and tried to keep any snide comments about the play to myself.

Tryouts went well, and she was called back to read again for the part of Abigail, which made her very hopeful. (Oh, and if you are wondering ... no, I did not do any magick in regards to her tryouts. I kept my magickal fingers out of this situation, thank you very much. We had enough drama going on.)

A week later, when the cast was announced, she was ultimately disappointed. She did not get a part in the play, after all. Seems the director's kid got the lead. Ah, nepotism is alive and well. When she told me about the cast posting, I felt badly that my daughter was so disappointed, but honestly I was also relieved. In an attempt to cheer her up, we went out to dinner and took in a movie. A few days later, things went back to whatever passes for normal at our house.

I thought it was important to illustrate that no, my life is not full of faerie wings, harp strings, and pixie dust. I deal with the same problems with my teens that other practitioners deal with. And there are times in your life when you have to take a step back from your magick and let things work themselves out, as in this situation with my daughter.

Tossing magick in the mix would have only complicated matters, especially with all the tempers and strong emotions that were involved. Sometimes you say a little prayer to the Lord and Lady, stand back, trust in that loving environment that you have nurtured them in, and wait to see how things unfold. We are often so busy as Witches working to make change in our lives that we forget there are times to believe in our kids and to take things on faith.

I felt it was essential to give my daughter some space and some time to let her come to terms with her religion and magick all on her own during her senior year of high school. When all was said and done, she was more confident in her beliefs and herself. To my amazement, as she packed up for college in the fall her Bast cat-goddess statue and a few magickal books went along to the dorm. She also made a request for me to put together a few candle-free spells so she could work them discreetly while living on campus, which I promised to do.

Teens are like plants sometimes. We watch them bud, sprout, and grow, amazed at how quickly they are evolving and becoming young adults. There are cycles and seasons of growth to be respected here. So give them a helping hand when it's needed. Nudge them into a better place with loving discipline, which is like pruning away things that are unnecessary, and at other times offer a sort of parental fertilizer, which is a mixture of love, respect, encouragement, and praise.

In a few short years, you will stand back and marvel at how they've matured and grown. Then finally you can begin to enjoy the blossoming of a new adult member into the family and into your life. For parents, these teenage years pass swiftly by—just like magick. So remember to love your kids, enjoy the journey, and try and keep a good sense of humor.

Chapter 7

When people go to work, they shouldn't have

to leave their hearts at home.

BETTY BENDER

Witchery at Work

Our jobs are a huge part of our everyday lives. Whether you work in an office, medical center, restaurant, factory, retail store, or anywhere else for that matter, there are many different kinds of magick, spells, and subtle psychic maneuvers that will positively influence the atmosphere at your job. Instead of just performing band-aid magick, consider employing them regularly so things run smoothly on a daily basis. By band-aid magick, I mean that you let things go until there is a problem, and then you scurry around trying to slap a spell here and there to cover up or to fix things. That's never good.

I believe that it's time for us as magickal practitioners to think about this scenario from a fresh perspective. Why not use our intuition and tap into that individual power? This will help make any witchery at work more potent, personal, and—of course—practical. After all, we spend at least a quarter of our day at our jobs anyway, so let's look at some fresh ways to enchant our working environments.

The power of color is one of those skills that as we learn, grow, and advance in the Craft, we tend to dismiss. *Well, I mean really,* you huff to yourself in annoyance, *I had my magickal color associations down cold in my first year . . .*

But guess what? There are levels and layers to Witchcraft and to magickal knowledge. Do you utilize the subtleties of color magick in your daily working life? Or do you forget about it until your back is against the wall and then you pull out all the witchy stops? No, I'm not talking about candle colors—I'm speaking of the colors that you wear and display on your own body—as in the clothes that are in your wardrobe.

> *Common sense is genius dressed*
> *in its working clothes.*
> R. W. EMERSON

THE JOB, THE WITCH, AND THE WARDROBE

I have written about the practical use of color before, in both the home and the garden. But this time, we have a much more personal use for this magickal information. Your personal power is "colored" by the garments that you dress in. Color has been proven to affect people's moods and their reactions to each other, and it makes a considerable psychic impression on other people. Truthfully, they may have no conscious knowledge of why it affects them, but it certainly does. This is a handy advantage to have and to use to your own benefit. Plus, the clever use of color in your wardrobe brings a whole new meaning to the phrase "dressing for success."

The following clothing shades are listed in color-wheel order. Compare these colors and hues to your current personal wardrobe, and see what your work clothes and accessories (ties, scarves, jewelry, or shoes) are telling others about you on an intuitive level.

You don't have to run out and buy a whole new wardrobe; be practical, and use the tools that are available to you. If you want to pull in a touch of color magick at work, make the appropriate changes affordably with accessories or key pieces, such as a scarf, tie, sweater, or shirt.

You could also be very discreet and use the following color magick information on a very personal level—where you know it's there, but no one else will. Consider magick-ally colored lingerie, stockings, socks, and underwear. You will find at the end of this catalog of colors a section on enchanting natural fabrics and how they can also affect your psychic and magickal energy flow. So take a good look at what's in your current wardrobe and conjure up a bit of colorful wardrobe magick.

BROWN—This is a warm, comforting color that grounds and helps quiet a mind that won't turn off. It is also a very nonthreatening color. Brown is linked to the element of earth, just as you'd expect, and is a fabulous warm and sooth-ing color.

BURGUNDY—A mixture of both powerful red and protective black, this is a color with a lot of oomph, and is one of those colors that is often over-looked. Shades of burgundy and maroon will actually protect you from the effects of certain types of needy and very emotionally draining people. Plus it wards off the occasional psychic vampire.

MAUVE—Mauve is a gorgeous color that encourages intuition and lessens men-tal confusion and the sensations of being overwhelmed by other stronger personalities. It also will help you gain cooperation from your coworkers. Mauve is actually a lighter tone of burgundy, so you can apply the qualities of burgundy in a lesser degree to this shade as well.

PINK—This shade reduces stress, relaxes its wearer, and is a soothing and receptive color. But this color is not just for the ladies—while it invokes very soft, fuzzy feelings when worn on a woman, if you are a male who occasionally wears a pink shirt, offset that color with a navy or burgundy tie, and it will project that you are a compassionate, relaxed individual who is secure and confident in his own style.

RED—There is something about red that just stops traffic (pun intended). There is the classic "I'm in charge" red suit for women, and the red power tie for the guys. This is a passionate and dynamic color. Associated with the element of fire and strong, intense emotions, this is the hue to go for when you want and expect your coworkers' full attention. See yourself as vibrant, strong, and intense; add a little red to your wardrobe, and see what happens!

ORANGE—Orange punches up its wearer with confidence, energy, and enthusiasm. There are many gorgeous shades of orange, so choose the most flattering one for your skin tones. Wear orange to garner all the success you deserve and boost your self-assurance and personal energy level while you are at it.

CORAL—This is a high-voltage combination of hot pink and bright orange. Coral is an extremely assertive color, as it gives its wearer the impression of confidence and approachability. This is a great color to wear in a meeting when you are nervous but determined and still want to present yourself in the best possible light.

YELLOW—Wearing yellow to work brings a bit of sunshine into your day, as it will promote personal vitality and brighten your mood as it reduces depression. This sunny color is linked to the element of air, so as you'd expect, it also promotes communication and the flow of ideas. Yellow makes your professional talents shine to their best advantage.

NEON GREEN—Neon green is still a popular color; however, I suggest using it in moderation at work, unless you want to really stand out. And if that is the case, go for it! Bright and glowing shades of apple, lime, and neon green will stimulate you and keep you fired up; they also encourage new business opportunities.

GREEN—The primary shade of green is for promoting career objectives while bringing prosperity, good luck, growth, health, and strength. This color promotes heart chakra energy—no surprise there—and is the color of life. It also helps keep you gently grounded and is an excellent link to the earth and all of its magick.

TURQUOISE—A mystical mixture of green and blue, turquoise is a fabulous color for healing, protection, and relieving stress. It's a great shade to wear when you need to pull up strength from deep inside yourself.

BLUE—This soft, healing shade can work wonders in a witchy wardrobe, as long as you don't go overboard with it. Blue represents the element of water, emotions, and psychic receptivity. Shades of pastel blue to denim can make you seem more open-minded and trustworthy—someone to confide in. It also helps you appear nonthreatening and will assist you in blending in and not drawing attention to yourself. However, if you wear too much blue, you may notice that you are feeling "blue" yourself, damn near invisible, or a little down in the dumps. So: all things in moderation, and remember to mix things—and your color palette—up.

ROYAL BLUE—I think of this shade as electric, and this color is also commonly known as electric blue. It is a strong and dynamic color. Need a boost? Try working a bit of exciting royal blue into your work wardrobe. Associated with the prosperous planetary energies of Jupiter, this is the color for the movers and shakers. It grabs attention, is a forceful color, and can be very uplifting, protective, and powerful.

DARK BLUE/ NAVY—This color is a mixture of blue and black, and it does inspire respect and confidence. Interestingly, it also creates the impression of emotional distance—the exact opposite of what the softer tones of blue will create—so bear that in mind.

LAVENDER—A relaxing color, this tint brings out your inner beauty and is a calming color to wear in the middle of a crisis or deadline. Lavender shades provide the subtle undercurrents of the element of water. This color encourages tranquility and may help to counteract a jealous coworker.

PURPLE—A favored color for magick users. The most royal of shades, it promotes fame, riches, respect, spirituality, and power. This shade also promotes inspiration and imagination. There are many shades of purple available, so again, choose the most flattering tone to complement your own coloring, and follow your instincts.

SILVER—This shimmering color promotes self-respect and spirituality. It can help reduce fears, while bumping up a feeling of safety and security. This is a Goddess color, and it is a motivational and receptive hue. If wearing a silver lamé blouse isn't your thing, consider silver jewelry.

GREY—Illusion, neutrality, and glamour; this color promotes invisibility. If all hell is breaking loose at work and your boss is on the warpath this week, then grey is the way to go. It's not the only use, however. Grey is a good neutral color. And if you are comfortable in your grey skirt or slacks, then punch it up with a colored shirt, tie, or scarf and add a bit more color magick to the mix.

WHITE—A teaching and healing color—think doctors and nurses. Unless it is a part of your uniform, for best results, wear white in small amounts, otherwise it is overpowering. To be honest, there are very few people—unless they are super-thin runway models—who look good in a lot of white. So try a shirt, blouse, or sweater. To warm up mystical white and its effects, try a soft, warm shade of ivory.

BLACK—This hue conjures up images of power, intrigue, and mystery. It lets folks know that you are in a position of authority. It is also a very fashionable and dynamic color for most people—think black tuxes and suits for men, or the black cocktail dress or a long, flowing, witchy ebony skirt for the women. Show me a Witch that doesn't have at least one all-black outfit! The color black establishes boundaries; it also can create a type of color shield, if you are the type to have your feelings hurt easily. Consider adding some black clothes to your wardrobe; depending on the cut and style, it can be used to attract attention or to deflect it. The choice and the power to wield that type of color magick is up to you.

FASCINATING NATURAL FABRICS

Fabrics also influence the flow of magick in your life. Not surprisingly, clothing made from natural fibers is the best energy conductor. Since polyester and rayon are man-made, they aren't going to conduct energy and magick on their own. It's sort of like expecting an artificial flower to hold any magickal energy. Keep that in mind when you get dressed for work in the morning, or before you choose the fabric for your next ritual outfit.

The following textile information is simple, straightforward, and very self-explanatory. Bear in mind the way you react to certain textures in fabric. Does slipping on a favorite pair of denim blue jeans help you unwind, or does denim make you feel like you are ready to do yard work? Does wearing a wool blend suit help you feel more professional while at the office, or does wool make you itchy and uncomfortable? Cotton allows energy to flow or breathe, which makes sense as it is a breathable fabric. Cotton also increases your clarity and is associated with the element of (you guessed it) air. Wool is an earthy fabric; it is considered formal and protective, sturdy and secure.

Silk is the most magickal of all fabrics. When worn, silk creates a one-way psychic mirror. This material is protective and shields whatever it covers from outside influences and psychic energy. This is why it was always considered correct to wrap tarot cards in silk—to shield them from other people's emotions and vibes. So if it will protect and shield tarot cards, imagine what it can do for you. I have read that silk is not considered appropriate for the office, as it is too sensual or suggestive. Bah! I'd say that is completely up to you. A gorgeous silk blouse paired up with a nice suit would be stunning, in my opinion. Or you could be really discreet and wear silk underwear; that ought to put you in a good mood all day.

Silk is linked to your emotions, intuition, and the element of water, which isn't a big surprise, as this fabric "flows" across the body. Also FYI, a silk tie can even be used as a sort of psychic shield for businessmen, as a tie lays directly in front of your heart and solar plexus chakras. There it provides a shield from the negativity of others as it keeps your own power centers protected, so you don't fall victim to personal draining tactics. And everyone knows there is always one idiot in the office who seems to suck the life and energy right out of the room—or you. So enchant that silk tie or blouse, choose the color carefully, and think of it as subtle and very effective mirrored psychic armor.

Colorful Clothing Conjuration

With all our discussion on colors and fabrics in your wardrobe, here is a spell to coordinate with the information that will help you enchant the clothes you wear to work. To begin, choose the colors and fabrics of your outfit with your intention utmost in your mind, such as to project an aura of power, to boost your own confidence, or to blend in and go unnoticed at work. Whatever your goal is, picture it and keep that vision firmly in mind as you choose your outfit carefully. Once your magickal goal is set, then get dressed, finish the rest of your grooming for the day, and stand in front of your mirror.

Stand up straight, and take a good look at yourself. Then you should say something positive—a declarative statement like one of the following affirmations:

- Today I work with the powerful energy of the color red to manifest success.
- Today I utilize the gentle energy of the color blue and will be more open-minded, sympathetic, and compassionate.
- Today I harness the power of the color yellow; may it bring illumination and boost my communication skills.
- Today I work with the magick of the color black; I build my shields with strength and reject my coworkers' power to make me uncomfortable.

(Remember to refer to the discussion on colors beginning on page 149 to customize this spell to suit your personal needs.) After you have made your opening statement, visualize light and energy flowing around you and wrapping you up in its strength. You may notice that you feel a bit warmer or experience a tightening at the solar plexus area. That's fine; just keep going. When you are ready and are feeling that you have woven the magick around yourself snugly, then repeat the following verse:

As it is within, now so without,

Circle the magick 'round and about.

Fabrics of cotton, wool, and silken strings,

Weave around me now while success you bring.

By color and my will, this spell I cast,

May it create change that surely lasts.

Finally, take a deep breath in. Hold it for a count of four. Let it out slowly and center yourself. Now flash a cocky smile at your own reflection. You look fabulous! Head off to your job with confidence, secure in the knowledge of your personal and practical magick. Go get 'em!

Who is the Goddess,

and what's she doing in the office?

Z. Budapest

Influencing the Psychic Atmosphere at Work

I have yet to meet the person who hasn't dealt with some type of problem at their jobs. Over the years, I have personally had bosses I swore were either sociopaths, had multiple personalities, or were just certifiably insane. I've worked alongside friendly, easygoing employees and angry, mean, and petty coworkers. And so, I imagine, have most of you. Sometimes these dramas made me nervous or unhappy, and sometimes they just made me laugh.

Over the years, I learned to develop a few techniques that would influence the psychic atmosphere at work—and that was not always an easy task, especially in an office-type of environment or a large retail store, when working with different departments and numerous employees. So I had to learn to keep it subtle and to fine-tune my magick to the troublemaker and to my immediate workspace, wherever that happened to be.

Now, there were plenty of days where everything went smoothly, and no magick was necessary. And then there were days when I was ready to pull out my hair—not to mention the days when the people I worked with, employees and supervisors alike, would pounce on me the moment I walked in the door. They would follow me to my locker, with a hopeful look on their faces, and ask me to do something—anything—to settle down a troublesome manager.

At first, I thought my friends at work and fellow employees were just gently teasing me in sort of a friendly "Hey, we're cool with what you do" type of thing. But they were serious. When people find out they're working with a Witch, they expect you to fix these little situations, which at first surprised, then amused me. It's very difficult to keep a straight face when your coworkers tell you that votive candles are on sale in aisle three, ask what color you'll need for a spell, and then offer to buy them for you—all so you can get the psycho boss to chill out and to leave them alone.

Creating a Psychic Anchor

Here are some nifty tricks that you can easily do at work, as they are subtle enough that no one will know what you are doing. These can help you to protect your feelings, retain your composure, and to even keep a grip on your temper. These spells will come in handy when you work with an aggressive, combative type of personality or when you have to work in close proximity with an emotional or psychic vampire.

Remember that both types of negative personalities enjoy putting you at a disadvantage, either through fear or through draining the good mood, creativity, and positive energy right out of you. These folks are all about power; they want it all, and they don't have a qualm about sucking you dry. So if you are tired of being their midday snack, you need to change your reaction to them. Shifting your mood and the psychic energy you put out will accomplish this, as it will throw them off for a moment and allow you to throw up a psychic shield to protect yourself from any more abusive treatment or draining tactics.

A psychic anchor is a type of magickal trigger. This is a gesture that immediately will summon a positive reaction or emotion. Many people use these types of power gestures and never even realize it. Here is an example: placing the hand on the heart is a common gesture that folks often make to remind themselves to calm down or for comfort when they feel that they have just had a close call. It is a way to slow your speeding heart rate and it is a subconscious way of telling yourself to take a breath and to relax.

The trick here is to create a neutral gesture that you can do easily and without drawing a lot of attention to yourself, and then to practice it so it becomes second nature. When you work the hand gesture, you will be shifting your emotional state to one of serenity, composure, and peace.

First things first: choose a hand gesture. Some practical suggestions are crossing your fingers, touching the center of your forehead with the index finger, or even placing the palms of your hands together. You could also place your thumb and first finger together in a sort of relaxed "okay" type of hand sign—just don't flare out your other fingers, let them stay relaxed, curled close together, and natural.

Once you have chosen the trigger, make the hand gesture and relax so it can begin to trigger a different state of mind. Close your eyes, take a stabilizing deep breath in, and slowly release it. Repeat twice more. Now visualize that as you are performing these nice slow and controlled breaths, you are breathing in peace and tranquility and then blowing out the stress and bad vibes. Keep holding the hand gesture. This will help to "anchor" or program this physical act in your mind, so the psychic and emotional shift that you are going for occurs. Finally, say quietly to yourself:

I create peace and tranquility with this sign;

May it work for me in any place or any time.

Then open your eyes and allow yourself to come back to a physical awareness. You shouldn't have to ground and center, but if you think you need to, please do so. Open your hands, and allow them to relax. Practice this often so you can trigger the positive psychic response that you are looking for without giving in to anger.

Crafting Psychic Armor

I first wrote about this technique several years ago in my book *Elements of Witchcraft*, and it is a quick, no-fuss way to create that psychic armor. It has always worked well for me, my circle mates, and my students, in many situations. Imagine yourself encased in a big, bright blue sphere of light. I like to hold my arms out at my sides, with my palms out. (You can act like you are stretching, if you want to be discreet.) Then take in a big, strong breath, and say to yourself, "Shields up!" Then picture a bubble of light and protection closing around you with a soft "pop." Slowly let the breath out. Imagine this large, glowing sphere of light being large enough to surround you easily, both over your head and under your feet. Then gently lower your arms. This psychic protection shield can be enhanced by adding the following phrase:

As above, now so below;

All around me protection grows.

If the Witch's sphere of light seems too big or awkward for you to put together while you are at work, you can always try the following variations. You can visualize yourself in a medieval style of armor that glows electric blue, or you can create in your mind a circle of mist that coalesces and then wafts around you. With the mist visualization I like to picture a large, brewing, sapphire-colored cauldron at my feet. The contents of this deeply blue cauldron bubble, boil, and then spill over the sides.

As the liquid hits the ground, I imagine it forming a mist of glittery, blue-colored protection around me. Depending on the situation, the mist may spin clockwise or counter-clockwise; typically I see clockwise as protective and counter-clockwise as banishing, meaning that it typically "banishes" or removes any negative person right out of my workspace. While using this visualization, I have had negative people abruptly back away from me and then complain about how warm they suddenly are feeling.

Try these for yourself; after all, a Witch should always have a few clever tricks up their sleeves.

> *Look, there's no metaphysics on earth like chocolate.*
> FERNANDO PESSOA

WITCHY TRICKS AND TREATS

Never underestimate the power of baked goodies; simple, subtle, and very effective, they are the fastest way to positively change the atmosphere at work. This way you can spread a little positive influence and share the love—fudge brownies, chocolate chip cookies, or even fresh cinnamon rolls. By enchanting some homemade sweet treats, you allow them to bring happy and more friendly vibes to the work environment. You could go with the cinnamon rolls—cinnamon promotes protection and prosperity—but personally, I'd go for the chocolate. There is a reason it's called the "food of the gods," after all.

No doubt about it: chocolate is magickal. In fact, chocolate contains phenylethylamine, and this substance sets off a sensation in your body that is very much like that old "falling in love" feeling. Why? Well, when chocolate hits the taste buds, they are stimulated, and then endorphins are released—and that makes your body feel good. While researching the mystery of chocolate, I had to chuckle. There are some pretty serious medical articles about chocolate stating that there is "a link between hormonal fluctuations in women and chocolate cravings." What, have those guys been living in a cave? Hell yes, there is.

The good news is that chocolate isn't necessarily bad for you. It has less caffeine than most people think. There are just 10 milligrams of caffeine in the average chocolate bar, compared to a cup of coffee that has 100 milligrams. Chocolate is rich in magnesium and phosphorous, and it contains antioxidants. The darker and finer chocolate contains more potent antioxidants called phenols. Phenols, it seems, prevent bad cholesterol from building up in the arteries. So you can indulge in chocolate occasionally, and the world won't stop revolving.

Chocolate has the magickal correspondences of the planet Mars; hurray for warrior energy! It is also linked to the element of fire, so we can easily tap into that element to create "transformation." Plus chocolate encourages love and wealth. Well, there you go.

Have things at work been a little "off" lately? The following chocolate spell works well when you are usually happy at work but are noticing a lot of stress and unhappy coworkers. This is a practical type of magick, and it is a great way to stop your fellow employees from bickering and sniping at each other, as the spell transforms negative emotions and vibrations into positive, friendly ones.

A Chocolate Spell

To begin, conjure up something sweet and chocolatey to take to work. After it is baked, enchant the food so that when it is consumed, it instills a sense of camaraderie and happiness. This should help to bring a shift in the atmosphere at work. As the baked item cools, hold your hands over the treat and visualize a soothing pink light coming from your hands and swirling into the dish. Keep that goal of "changing the work atmosphere to a positive one" in your mind. Then repeat this charm:

> *They used to call chocolate the food of the gods,*
> *May this shift the psychic atmosphere at my job.*
> *Encourage happiness and friendship in a subtle way,*
> *Bringing efficiency and success for us all today.*
> *For the good of all, with harm to none,*
> *By these Witch's words, this spell is done.*

Now take the treat to work and leave it out in the break room with a note for everyone to enjoy it. This is subtle, effective magick, and nobody in their right mind passes up chocolate—unless they are evil. Okay, they might be allergic, but I'd be suspicious of them anyway. See if they cast a reflection, levitate, or foam at the mouth during lunch break, just to be sure.

There is nothing impossible in the existence
of the supernatural: Its existence seems
to me decidedly probable.
GEORGE SANTAYANA

MISSION: WICCA IMPOSSIBLE

It was during the middle of writing this book that I found myself in the position of having to go back to work. The winter holidays were coming up, and money was beyond tight. So I followed my instincts and went looking for a part-time job close to home. Four hours later, I had a job.

I was relieved to get this job: cute little shop, fairly pleasant boss, and a short drive to work. I was somewhat concerned about working outside the home again. It had been a year and a half, and at my last part-time job everyone there knew about my books and my religion, and to be honest nobody even batted an eye. (One of the nice things about working in a larger company.) However, working in a small boutique-type of atmosphere might be radically different. So I tucked in my pentagram necklace, dressed a bit more conservatively, and told myself to be a grownup and get over it. Because, after all, I wasn't getting a job for fun, I was working to help out with the family finances. The chances of someone recognizing me in this type of boutique environment were slim. The job was temporary; I knew it would only last through January—maybe February, if I was lucky. So I hoped for the best and went back to work.

On my first day at my job, I discovered that the owner's sibling worked at the shop too. And the sibling was a Fundamentalist Christian—a hard-core one at that. As I put away my purse, the sibling launched into a passionate tirade about this weird wedding that they had attended the night before. She was horrified because the bride's grandmother performed the ceremony and had tied the bride's and groom's hands together. As the previous evening had been Halloween, it was easy to guess she had attended a Pagan handfasting.

I clamped a hand over my mouth and walked into another room so I wouldn't laugh in front of them. I rolled my eyes to the ceiling, asked the Goddess to give me strength, and imagined that the Goddess was probably amused at my current situation, me being undercover and all, and enjoying the heck out of the show.

A few days later, my new boss began making some none-too-subtle inquiries about what my religious affiliations were, which I tap-danced around. I was funny and told her with a straight face that I was a free spirit and a modern, tree-hugging hippie (which confused her and bought me time). I was clever, I was entertaining, and I never answered a single question directly. At the end of my second harrowing week, I was on edge, on guard, and exhausted.

After a few more weeks, I settled in and finally found my sense of humor again. Now, it has been my experience that people tend to tell Witches the strangest things. Whether they even know about us or not, they tend to intuitively link in and feel that you are an open-minded soul, and therefore, you will listen to and offer advice on all their troubles. This theory of mine was put to a huge test at the end of my first month in the little shop of horrors. On that day, the store owner regaled me with the three-hour tale—nope, not an exaggeration, she talked about this for three freaking hours—how her life was saved by Jesus. Say that with a slight Southern accent, and you've got it: *Jeea-zus.*

I was told a tragic tale full of broken marriages, despairing children, and leaving one man for another only to be dumped several years later by her new man for a much younger woman.

"Whoa," I commented half under my breath as I tried to stay busy rearranging displays. "Can you say *karma?*"

"Can you say what?" My boss questioned suspiciously.

"Caramel," I said, deadpan. *Note to self: My inner monologue is broken.* On the fly, I smiled as I turned around and calmly replied, "Do you smell caramel?"

My boss sniffed the air, shook her head no, and on it went—for a total of three incredibly long and stressful hours.

At one point, I started to consider what the fastest way to end my suffering could be … Should I leap off the store's second-floor balcony, or just wait for my brains to start leaking out of my ears? The story was finally concluded with my boss explaining that they had even considered ending it all, because they were so disgusted with all the lives that they had ruined. Then, in a moment of glory, they became … drum roll, please … Christian.

Hey, I was two for two! It wasn't only the sibling who was a fundie, it was also my boss. Now the boss was on husband number three (or was it four?), and they were members of a very large local church, I was informed, one with television commercials and everything, and they were now spreading the good word and saving lives.

I mean, *what* are the odds? Good grief. Only I could end up in such a situation. By the time this story was finished, I was one wound-up and nervous Witch. I could not afford to make any waves or identify myself as a Witch. Keeping my mouth shut and not commenting on that tale was one of the hardest things I have ever done. Plus my natural sense of humor and sarcasm could really cause trouble here. Truth was, I needed this damn job. My family was counting on me, and it was too close to the holidays to find another one.

Finally I was able to escape this never-ending story and fled to the lower floor of the shop. One of the other employees took one look at me and immediately came over to pat me on the back in sympathy. When I briefly explained where I had been for the past three hours, they could only grimace and then offer to buy me a drink after work. Ah, so it wasn't just me who was being regaled with the story.

I called a Pagan friend that evening and talked to them about my situation. Okay, I whined, moaned, groaned, and complained about how hard it was to keep a low profile and to stay undercover. My friend was laughing hysterically and begging me to include this in the book.

"It's not funny!" I complained.

"It's great!" She howled with laughter. "Maybe, just maybe, you can teach those women something. They probably need a lesson in religious tolerance." My friend told me that perhaps the Goddess had plans for me—spiritual plans that I was simply unaware of at the present time. Maybe I was on a mission, my friend cheerfully pointed out.

"Yeah, *Mission: Wicca Impossible,*" I agreed with a grumble. But you have to admit—that is sort of catchy.

So here I was, a Witch undercover at work for the first time in years, working for an ultraconservative, fundamentalist boss. I could practically hear the theme music from *Mission: Impossible* every time I parked my car and then walked in the shop's back door. Once, when I was feeling particularly ornery, I slipped on my dark sunglasses and raced to the building. I flattened myself along the back brick wall and inched my way in slowly just for the dramatic effect.

There I was, skulking along the back wall, checking right and left, then diving into the door to slam it closed and lock it safely behind me. Was that mature? Absolutely not. But it did make me smile the rest of the day.

> *One morning I shot an elephant in my pajamas.*
> *How he got in my pajamas, I'll never know.*
> MORRIE RYSKIND

OPERATION PINK ELEPHANT

Just about the time I was congratulating myself for blending in and staying undercover, my master plan was neatly demolished. Now, my boss knew I wrote books; she just assumed they were on gardening. Do you recall the "Pink Elephant Syndrome" that was described for you in the last chapter? Yup, well, it also followed me to work. Those pink elephants are silent and sneaky! A few months after the holidays, I was on my way out the door to work one early February morning when I literally tripped over a flat package left on my doorstep. I flipped it over and saw that it was from the publishing company.

With no time to spare, I kept moving and tossed it in the car with my lunch, purse, and notebook, and then quickly drove to work.

After getting to work, I turned on the lights, counted the cash register, hung up my coat, and put my lunch in the fridge. Once I had the front door unlocked and the store open for business, I went behind the counter and opened the package: ooh, it was a nice surprise, too; it was the full cover art—front and back—for my book *The Enchanted Cat*. I had never received a full cover before for framing. As I looked it over, I was completely engrossed and completely oblivious to my boss, who let herself in the back door right behind me.

I calmly said good morning and went to slip the cover back in the box. There was unfortunately no way to be discreet, and I was already cursing myself for opening up the package at work. When my boss inquired about the artwork in my hand, I took a deep breath and handed her the cover art.

She commented on how pretty the artwork was and chuckled at the tabby cat. She's a huge cat fan herself. The boss made a nice comment about how exciting it all was and that she was looking forward to seeing the finished product at the bookstores in a few weeks. As she stood there and read the back cover copy, I kept a pleasant smile on my face while my heart pounded, and I thought, "Okay, this is it."

The words "Witch" and "Witchcraft" were in several spots on the back cover copy, as well as the author bio that says *Ellen Dugan, a practicing Witch for twenty years . . .*

She handed it back to me and suggested a good place to have the cover framed, and then I slipped it back in the box and set it aside. My boss gave me a list of things she needed accomplished that day, gave me her cell phone number in case I needed to reach her, and went about her business like nothing unusual had happened.

I let out a semi-relieved breath and figured she was probably freaking out downstairs with the other employees. But an hour later, she went to run her errands, and everything continued with no fuss at all. Hmm, maybe she didn't get it. After all, this is the same person who made up flyers to mail out for the shop and misspelled the word "huge" in the phrase "huge sale." All our flyers said "HUGH SALE"—and she mailed them out that way. I figured it might take a day or two to sink in. Feeling giggly and nervous, I picked up my cell phone and called one of my circle mates while they were at work.

As I heard her cheerful voice come across the line, by way of greeting I said seriously, "Operation Pink Elephant is a go."

Her answer was a loud snort of laughter, followed by a demand to tell her everything. She, too, was wondering if perhaps my boss either didn't pick up on it or if she was just pretending that it hadn't happened. Our best guess was that time would tell. We'd see how she reacted the next time I came to work.

And here's the interesting part: nothing was ever said. No rude or disparaging comments, no religious interventions, no cut hours; everything continued at work just as it always had. I worked at the store as seasonal help for several months and parted with my boss and fellow employees on very friendly terms. They even asked me if I'd be willing to come back and to lend a hand during their busiest time of the year.

So I had to ask myself, when all was said and done, just who the Goddess was giving a lesson to here. Perhaps I shouldn't be so defensive about my magickal faith and so quick to assume that just because someone was conservative, they would be intolerant of a faith different from their own. Who would have ever thought it? Certainly not me.

So there was a spiritual lesson to be learned from this job, after all. However, the one who needed to be taught religious tolerance the most was me.

A Prayer for Religious Tolerance

Lord and Lady, help me to set a good example as a Witch today.

Bless my body so that I may walk a path of wisdom.

Bless my heart; may it remain compassionate and loving.

Bless my mind so it can stay open and nonjudgmental.

For your magickal lessons are many, and kind and tolerant people

Do come from all backgrounds and religions.

Chapter 8

Personal example carries more weight than preaching.

CHINESE PROVERB

Spirituality and Personal Advancement

As we've seen, natural witchery is a magickal method that encourages you to trust in your intuition, embrace your personal power, and rejoice in your connection to nature. It also supports the idea of then combining all of the above and showing you how to live the magick in a practical way, each and every day.

How you as an individual draw strength from all of these aspects of your life—the intuitive, personal, and practical sides of magick—is a crucial part of your earth religion. Throughout this book, I have given you dozens of ways and shown you fresh ideas so you can put these methods to good use. We've worked our way through chapters on intuition and psychic development, personal growth and personal power, and we've studied the practical and psychic dynamics of group work. We've also taken a realistic look at another important part of your life in the Craft by discussing our living environments and the things that affect them, such as your family and your job. So to finish up this book, I thought it would be a good idea to discuss and explore a topic that we have yet to touch on, and that topic is spirituality.

Honestly, spirituality isn't a flowery concept to be tucked aside until it is convenient for you to consider. Your spirituality needs to be integrated into your daily life if it is to be a meaningful expression of who you are as a Witch. By continuing your search for information and knowledge, and by working on your personal improvement, you in turn become an adept or advanced magickal practitioner. When you take the time to look within and to see who you really are, you begin to grow and to change; in essence, you begin to blossom into a more spiritual person.

> *Let us be grateful to the people who make us happy;*
> *They are the charming gardeners*
> *who make our souls blossom.*
> MARCEL PROUST

TENDING TO OUR SPIRITUALITY

Tending to your own inner spirituality is like caring for a garden, and gardening is not for wimps. It always makes me smile to talk to a new gardener who is simply amazed at the sheer amount of work and hours they have to put in to keep a garden maintained, happy, and healthy. The same type of maintenance, hard work, and attention also applies to keeping our spirituality on track.

When it comes to spirituality, here the newer magickal practitioner has an edge on the more experienced one. Why? Because they still have boundless energy and enthusiasm for the magickal life. It's all new, exciting, and fresh to their eyes. Everything is magickal, and even ordinary, daily experiences take on an enchanting quality when seen through the eyes of a new Witch.

So, using this "nurturing your spirituality is like tending to a garden" analogy, let's explore this idea a little further. As is often the case, the longer you've been practicing the Craft, the easier it is to become a lazy spiritual gardener. You only take care of that divine garden when things go wrong and you have to fix them. As time goes by, you become so used to the magickal life that you often ignore the charming things that once were precious to you—which is not unlike ignoring the flowers until they are drooping with thirst, then quickly watering them so they pop back up, only to ignore them again until things start to look ragged. Think how much healthier those plants in our spiritual garden would be if they received regular attention and care. With regular maintenance, those pesky weeds or dilemmas would be at a minimum, and our plants or lives would grow stronger and be more resistant to troubles.

How many of you have ever tried to pull out a weed from the garden? It's so much easier to rip out the weed's roots if you hunker down and get closer to the earth. And here is another divine gardening lesson for you to consider: you can't pull those weeds (magickal or otherwise) while standing on the outside edge of the spiritual garden. You have to get in there and get those hands dirty! Feel the ground beneath you—it offers support and strength—and tug out those occasional weeds of negativity. Clip back that old, spent foliage of self-doubt. Come on, you can do it! Reconnect to the natural world, honor your intuition, and remember what it's like to experience the divine around you in simple and profound ways.

Care for your witchy self in the same way you would care for garden plants: with nourishment, time, and attention every single day. This makes for a happy and healthy spiritual garden and a strong, confident, and wise Witch. Cultivate both your spirituality and sense of enchantment by rediscovering the simple things that once delighted you, for when you nurture the magickal self, your spirituality blossoms.

> *True simplicity as a conscious choice*
> *illuminates our lives from within.*
> SARAH BAN BREATHNACH

LIVING THE MAGICK EVERY DAY

Living the magick on a daily basis can be somewhat of a challenge when you are surrounded by the demands and stress of day-to-day life. There are bills to pay, kids to haul to sports practice, dirty laundry, house cleaning, and the ever-popular teenage melodramas. I know that, for myself, after twenty years in the Craft there have been times when I began to feel a little disconnected. It usually sneaks up on me. I get so busy with the family, my writing, my job, and studying the magickal arts and taking them apart piece by piece so I can write about them and teach them that I forget to take a moment or two every day to celebrate the sacred.

So, how *do* you find the magickal in the mundane and uncover the sacred in the ordinary? Why, I thought you'd never ask. You simplify. The truth is, you already have inner wisdom and all the creativity you'll ever need to make magick in your life; you just may be too busy to notice it. Well, here is your big chance. Quiet your mind, listen to your heart, and look within.

The trick is to set some time aside for yourself to nurture your own spirituality. Remember the spiritual garden we discussed before? This is the where the maintenance comes in. Begin by keeping things basic and simple. It's an interesting truth that the longer you've been practicing the Craft, the more uncomplicated your magick becomes. That's because you have learned what works the best for you.

So before you start to think that only a lengthy, complicated ritual process is the mark of an experienced Witch, be realistic. Simplicity for the veteran Witch is like a breath of fresh air. Now that we have your intuition humming along, get back to the basics and remember what it was like to rejoice in the most practical and essential of magickal techniques.

A Little Natural Witchery Elemental Homework

Here are a few simple suggestions for you to consider; these will help you sense the magick that swirls around you in your environment, as well as remind you to keep those elemental personality qualities that we worked on earlier nicely in balance. Go outside on a pleasant day, and feel the breeze as it blows past you. Now take a moment and acknowledge it as the element of air sending positive change on the winds. Work with that energy so you can communicate your thoughts clearly and so you are inspired and knowledgeable.

Watch the sun rise, and notice carefully the colors that paint themselves across the sky. The sun is a natural representation for the element of fire, so start paying attention to the colors and the force of the sun and the power of light that illuminates your days. Tap into this luminous energy and become inspired, passionate, and strong.

Take a quick trip to the nearest natural body of water, whether it is a creek, lake, river, or ocean. Stand safely along the banks or shoreline, and see what different energies you personally notice there. Whenever I am stressed out, I head to a local riverfront park and find a nice park bench, take some personal time, and just silently watch the Missouri River go by. It never fails to clear my head, and it also gives me a chance to get rid of any anger or frustration that I am holding on to. The natural energies of the water element can help you to wash away stress and discontent. While you are there enjoying the view, take advantage of the soothing and healing qualities of water, soak up a little positive atmosphere, and clear your heart and mind.

Go to a park on your lunch break, and sit beneath the shade of a tree. Or just take a seat on the grass in your own backyard. Feel the ground beneath you, and take some time to really ground and center. You could wrap your arms around a tree trunk and experience the life force within. Use this experience to connect to the solid and steady magick that is a blessing from the earth. Call on this earthy magick for protection and security, and to keep your personal prosperity flowing.

Finally, watch the moon rise some night on your own porch, and feel the gentle illumination of the Goddess as she sends her blessings down to you. Tip up your face to the moon's silver light and improvise a quick prayer of thanks for all the wonderful things that you have in your life. Dare to take some personal time just for yourself to celebrate your spirituality and to enjoy your earth religion!

More things are wrought by prayer
than this world dreams of.
ALFRED, LORD TENNYSON

A WITCH'S PRAYER

Prayer is both a simple and a profound method to help you find your way while traveling along your own sacred path. When a Witch uses prayer as a magickal tool, it gives them a little one-on-one time with the God and Goddess. This is a phenomenal and very personal way to experience a connection to the divine. Prayer can be both spur-of-the-moment and a part of your regular spiritual practices. Plus it is an intimate technique to express your own spirituality. The act of setting aside some personal time to say a prayer is a beautifully simple ritual.

Connecting with deity through the use of prayer gives a natural Witch inner strength. Prayer is one of the most time-effective and practical ways to revitalize your magickal spirituality, especially if you've been feeling overwhelmed and disconnected. In fact, a Witch's prayer can open up a doorway between the psychic realms and the magickal realms, because when we acknowledge the enchanting moments of our lives with a simple magickal prayer, we get in touch with our feelings, honor our intuition, and tune in to the realms of the spirit all at once!

A Witch's prayer is like a spontaneous spell. Truthfully, it all depends on the amount of psychic energy that is raised and the quantity of will that is projected into the spoken prayer. A Witch's prayer can actually be an act of natural magick in and of itself; no waiting, no tools, just *boom*—and there it is.

Now, I realize that many Pagans will shy away from the use of prayer. They think it's too much like a mainstream religious practice. But all religions use prayer of some type. Praying doesn't involve groveling before deity. It's about building a relationship and going to deity when things get tough. How many of you have ever had to face down a tough situation and said quietly to yourself, as you walked into the confrontation, "Okay, Goddess, help me to handle this situation well" or "Lord and Lady, give me strength to deal with my teenagers today." Those are spontaneous prayers.

The spoken word has power. The soul opens up with simple invocations that honor the God and Goddess, life, and love. Remember that there is more to a prayer than just saying, "Please give me this item …" or "I really need that …" A prayer is also about thanking deity for their blessings and for their assistance in your spiritual life. And that's just one idea. You may also wish to recognize deity and celebrate the elements for their assistance in your magick at a specific time every day, like when you get up in the morning or before you turn in at night.

Now, it is important to be spontaneous and to use your own words while putting together these Witch's prayers. But I do understand that some folks absolutely panic at the thought of writing their own spells, or any magickal material, for that matter. So here are a few formal magickal prayers to get you motivated and inspire you to compose a few of your own.

To Honor the Moon Goddess

This Witch's prayer is for celebrating one aspect of the Goddess. The moon goddess is a powerful archetype, and this prayer will work well no matter what phase the moon happens to be in. All you need for this is yourself and a clear view of the moon. If you really wanted to go all out, you could light a white or silver candle at the beginning of this prayer. When you are finished, allow the candle to burn in a safe place until it goes out on its own.

> *Lady of the silver moon, watch over me this night,*
> *Guide my words and actions, and keep me within your sight.*
> *I thank you for your love and for protecting me from strife,*
> *I honor you for bringing charm and magick to my life.*

To Honor the God of Nature

This Witch's prayer honors the God as the Green Man and the spiritual side of nature. The Green Man is a popular, powerful aspect of the God and a favorite among most Witches today. If possible, try praying this outdoors in your backyard or garden. If you live in the city, try saying this spell while under a tree or walking through the local park. Or set aside a spot in your home, and fill it with several live houseplants, thus creating a indoor oasis of sorts. If you are working this prayer at home and can keep a small candle supervised, add a green candle to this prayer if you desire.

> *The smiling Green Man, soul of nature, now hear my call today,*
> *You manifest within my life in many wonderful ways.*

Please grant me compassion and strength, and help me to be wise.

Thank you for illumination beneath your sunny skies.

If you are wondering where the correct place is to work these formal Witch's prayers, that is completely up to you. But since I am a huge advocate of natural magick, personally I would suggest the outdoors, under the light of the sun or moon. If you are limited to an indoor area, then at least move to a place where you'll stand in a beam of natural light, because natural light has a power all its own. The light of the sun and moon has traditionally been recognized as an essential type of spiritual illumination. Surprise! There is truly magick to be found in the most simple of things.

A Celebration of the Magickal Elements

In natural magick, the elements of earth, air, fire, water, and spirit are called upon and utilized all the time. After all, we work with the elements every time we cast a circle. So why not take a moment to celebrate them and to thank them for the energies they bring to your natural witchery? This is a powerful and personal way to recognize all the positive and spiritual qualities they bless us with every day.

If you'd like to add a candle to this prayer, try white, since it's all-purpose. Or you could really get into it and use several candles: a green candle for earth, yellow for air, red to denote fire, blue for water, and purple for spirit. Set up this spell on your indoor working space or just step outdoors, ignore the props, and instinctively link to nature. Repeat the following prayer out loud and with feeling:

I thank the earth for its grounding and prosperous qualities,

I thank the air for the insight and knowledge it grants to me.

I thank the fire for passion and courage both true and bold,

I thank the water for psychic gifts and love to have and hold.

Thanks to Spirit, the element that binds all powers as one,

Now as I will it, so must it be, and bring harm to none.

Let your religion be less of a theory
and more of a love affair.
G. K. CHESTERTON

FINDING THE SACRED IN THE ORDINARY, DISCOVERING THE MAGICK IN THE MUNDANE

Now that you've tried out a few Witch's prayers, let's take the idea of maintaining our spirituality even further. To be happy and at peace, you need to be thankful for the wonderful things in your life. Nah, I'm not talking about "If only I had that brand-new sports car/could jet off to the seashore for the weekend/could have a designer outfit, I'd be so happy…"

Oh please, let's be realistic here. I'm a practical woman and a very practical Witch. What I'm talking about are the little things that are actually the most important things:

your health, friends, home, and family. I want to remind you to cherish these things because they are vitally important to keeping your spirituality on track.

If you are moping around, feeling blue or sorry for yourself, it's going to be a tall order for you to see the sacred and feel spiritual, much less magickal. So, what do you do? Well, you can try keeping a personal journal of sorts, and write down what you cherish and are thankful for. You can use this as a personal exercise and note the enchanting and inspiring events that you experience in your life. This could even become a little daily ritual, if you like; to look for and then to find the sacred in the ordinary.

Take the time to note the things or people that you most appreciate. Choose five different things that you are thankful for on a daily basis, and write those down. Something like this: *I am thankful for my job, so I can help support my family.* See? It's a positive affirmation, and it only took a moment of your time. Now try adding four more things to that list. For example, if I were to do this right now, I'd say:

1. Today I am thankful for my and my husband's good health.
2. I am thankful for my kids, Goddess bless them. They make me laugh and learn.
3. I am thankful I was able to afford putting in a new kitchen floor this year. It's so much easier to keep clean.
4. I am thankful for my cats; they bring me companionship every day.
5. I am thankful for our home and our garden.

The point of this is to help remind you what wonderful things you are blessed with. You may have noticed I have listed a kitchen floor. Work with me here: *sacred in the or-*

dinary, magickal in the mundane ... To you that may not seem magickal or particularly inspiring, but to me it was a huge deal. I purchased that floor tile with money earned from the magickal books I have written, so it was an epic event for me.

I enjoyed the whole process immensely. Having my oldest son take me to the home-improvement store with his truck so we could haul the tile home ... Getting to whip out my checkbook to pay for the whole thing myself ... my husband and I taking a weekend to lay the tile ourselves. It was hard work, but it was most satisfying. Not only does the whole kitchen look better, but it also looks bigger and brighter. Every time I walk in there, it just lifts my spirits and reminds me that I am contributing to help care for our home and help support my family.

Acknowledging the positive things in your life is an affirmative and powerful thing. It keeps you optimistic and reminds you to be thankful, whether you are thankful for a new kitchen floor, are cherishing a loving relationship, are appreciative of a loving home environment, or are simply taking pleasure in planting a flower garden in your yard or a pot of herbs for spells. Enjoy them all. There is magick to be found all around you, and there is a sacred and spiritual side to your everyday life. It's up to you to pay attention and to discover it. And it doesn't stop there. Jot down any important events in your life, and note the little things that inspire you. See what you can learn about yourself as you go along.

Today a new sun rises for me; everything is animated,

everything seems to speak to me of my passion,

everything invites me to cherish it.

ANNE DE LENCLOS

DAILY DOSE OF INSPIRATION

The fastest way for a Witch to be spiritually or magickally motivated is to get the physical senses involved. What simple things in the natural world inspire you? Watching the sun rise over the ocean, feeling crisp autumn leaves crunch under your shoes? Does the boom and crash of a thunderstorm rev you up? Do you become moved by the scent and texture of flowers or stirred by the earthy fragrance of the forest?

Inspiration may arrive in myriad ways; what counts is that you cherish it when you find it. Sometimes you have to snap yourself out of the doldrums and get in there and pull those choking weeds from the spiritual garden. This happens to all of us. The flowers are being smothered, and you need to get some air and inspiration to the plants in that spiritual garden!

For example, a few years ago I was having trouble finding inspiration to finish a writing project, and I was feeling particularly down in the dumps. I sat on the living room couch one afternoon in the foulest of moods. As I tried to identify what the problem was, I discovered that I had been spending an awful lot of time indoors on the computer, slaving away.

Consequently, I felt sluggish, disconnected from nature, and burned out. I took a moment and searched my intuition and asked myself what I needed to do to get pumped back up again. *Go outside, now,* my intuition announced. After a second or two, I decided that even though it was hot, getting outside and doing something beat the hell out of sitting on the couch and moping.

I shook myself off, clipped my hair up on top of my head, and then headed outside with my gardening tools and gloves, looking for inspiration. If inspiration was to be found, I knew I'd find it in the garden. So I determinedly hunkered down to weed the front flower beds. My husband was also outside cutting the grass, and as usual, getting in the gardens soothed me. So I pulled weeds, sweated, deadheaded the spent blossoms, got dirty, sweated some more, and tidied up the flowers. While I was in the gardens (looking very glamorous, I'm sure), a trio of late-summer butterflies fluttered around me as I worked. I also noticed a few hummingbirds zipping about. Cheered, I enjoyed their company, ignored the heat, and felt my mood lift.

As I dumped the weeds in the compost pile, I realized that if I had still been inside, I wouldn't have enjoyed the pretty black and blue butterflies or the gorgeous hummingbirds. Actually, the more I thought about it, I began to realize that a hummingbird is a symbol of joy, and the butterfly is an emblem of transformation. The butterfly's colors of black and blue could even symbolize the removal of negativity and peace. Well, well. Wasn't that interesting?

On my way back to the front yard, I detoured inside and got my husband and I both some water. As I walked over to him, he turned off the lawn mower, and we stood there chatting for a moment. I remember standing there and thinking that I needed to pay more attention to the magickal messages that spirit was sending. After he finished his water, I turned to take the glasses back in the house, and I heard him shout.

I spun around just in time to see a big, gorgeous red-tailed hawk zip down at shoulder level, right between where he and I were standing. We see hawks flying around our old suburban neighborhood often, but never *that* close. There wasn't more than six feet between the two of us when it swooped down, less than five feet from the ground and almost close enough to touch. We both began to laugh in amazed delight as the hawk flew up high and circled the yard, only to land in the top of our big oak tree. The hawk perched there regally for a while, looking down on us with a superior attitude. I guess the hawk thought he'd give us a thrill, and he certainly did.

Messages, I realized. The hawk is a bringer of spiritual messages. When the hawk shows up, the element of spirit is thought to be on the job and sending you information about yourself and your life. I would have never received all these wonderful messages from nature if I would have ignored my intuition and stayed inside feeling sorry for myself. That experience left me jazzed for a good week afterwards. It was a wonderful present that my husband and I cherish. We still talk about the hawk that gave us a fly-by.

A religion without the element of mystery
would not be a religion at all.
Edwin Lewis

The Fifth Element: Spirit

Are you open to the messages that the element of spirit may be sending you? These messages from the spirit may be inconspicuous, or they can be about as subtle as a brick to the forehead. Living your life as a Witch means that you need to pay attention and keep watch for those spiritual messages, no matter what life may throw at you. Yes, I am speaking through personal experience here. I am not some type of Super Witch, and I don't write down all these suggestions and techniques to help you find a way to improve your spirituality and your own Witchcraft with the lofty attitude of "Well, of course, such a thing would never happen to me …" Oh, please. I share my own experiences because I believe that people relate to a personal story much more than they relate to dry instructions or eye-crossing theories.

So, what about the fifth and final element, the element of spirit? It is easy to focus on the traditional four elements of earth, air, fire, and water. They are the most familiar to us, and it is vitally important to have those four elemental energies working in harmony in your life. Once you have acknowledged this and make strides toward becoming a balanced person, you gain magickal confidence. However, if you really want to turn up the volume on your magick, the fifth element—spirit—can show you the way.

Spirit is the life force that the other elements are born from. Spirit is represented as the top point of the pentagram and found at the center of a circle. It is above and below, and within as well as without. This element corresponds to every zodiac sign. It can be a physical presence that surrounds you or something ethereal and fleeting. Spirit is both masculine and feminine; it is all colors, all seasons, and the energy found in daily life. It can also be an elusive quality to capture, like trying to catch the wind inside of a paper bag. It is a paradox.

Now, if you are wondering just why this element is so tricky to define and so darn hard to physically "grab hold of," the best answer that I can give you is because this fifth element known as spirit is a mystery.

A mystery? I can just hear you grinding your teeth in frustration. No, I am not trying to sound all spooky and mysterious. The best way I can think to explain this to you is to give you an analogy: understanding the mysteries of the Craft is like becoming a parent. Oh, sure—in theory, a parent-to-be understands babies, and children, and how to raise them. After all, they have love for their child and the examples of friends and family to guide them. They read a few books, follow the example of other parents that they admire, and they listen to "the experts," so they feel that they are ready and know what to expect. Then they bring baby home, and guess what? Everything they *thought* they knew doesn't mean squat.

For every child is different, and every parenting situation is unique. The only way to earn your stripes as a parent is to raise the baby. By the time you have survived nighttime feedings, teething, crawling, and walking, then there is potty training and preschool. You look back on what you thought you knew about parenting and begin to realize there is so much more to understand. But hey, you love your kids, and you just know that you can handle anything. Just about the time you are patting yourself on the back, their primary school years begin. The next thing you know, they are playing sports, taking dance, and worrying about being cool. Then, Goddess help you, they morph into teenagers, and then you have to teach them how to drive and get them through high school and then off to college. By the time you are done, you look back and realize just how far you have come as a parent and how much you have grown as a person.

So can this "mysterious" and lengthy process really be explained to a new parent? Well, yes and no. You can certainly pass along some information and share the knowledge, but when it comes down to it, only time and living will give a new parent wisdom. The same can certainly be said of the Craft. So realize that this magickal development does take time and living. This is an on-the-job magickal training program, and it is one that lasts for a lifetime.

Look, between the stones is a blade of grass;

And all the rites of the High Mysteries,

And the runes of all witcheries,

Are written upon it.

DOREEN VALIENTE

TRAVELING THE PATH OF THE MYSTERIES

When it comes to the mysteries, I can certainly give you some pointers and nudge you in the correct direction of which path to travel, but when it comes to your relation with the divine and how you connect to the element of spirit, you will be walking this path on your own. For all Pagans, Wiccans, and Witches, the journey is every bit as important as the destination.

Craft knowledge is one thing; I am sure you can rattle off correspondences and theories just as well as the next Witch. However, to grasp the concept of spirit, you will require more than book learning. This quest is about taking the knowledge that you have gained as you travel your spiritual path and then turning it into wisdom. Truthfully, it is worth saying again, you do achieve real magickal wisdom by living your life, growing in your craft, and experiencing the natural cycles and seasons of growth and change.

By incorporating the aspect of spirit into your Witchcraft, you will move on to the next level of expertise. I have yet to meet any Witch who didn't want to become a more advanced magickal practitioner. The title "advanced Witch" always sounded sort of self-important to me; I prefer the word "adept." What I find very interesting is that the term "adept" is defined as someone who is "thoroughly proficient." Let's hear it for proficiency—which is another word for expertise—for the desire to advance your magickal skills and your witchery is a beautiful thing. And it is completely up to you.

To be a skilled or adept natural Witch is to be a practitioner who has an aptitude for the Craft, a flair and a real instinct for magick. These all can be improved by working with your intuition, by considering your own personal development, and by expanding your magickal skills until they become second nature. Your skill level will be enhanced by study, practice, and simply living the magick. (And if you've been paying attention, you have already figured out that that is just what we've been doing throughout this entire book.)

Well, what a lovely surprise. See, you have been improving your skills and working toward personal advancement all at once. Congratulations! The adept natural Witch works in harmony with the elements and nature, and they create their own personal and unique types of spells, charms, and magick. They also know when it's appropriate to work their magick and when it's best to stand back and to allow situations to unfold all on their own. An adept understands that in order to truly consider themselves a wise and skilled practitioner, they must have many years of experience under their belts. With time comes experience and wisdom. These folks happily contribute their personal time and talents to their community, and most importantly, an adept Witch sets a spiritual example for others to follow.

Essentially, an adept natural Witch is a confident one. Adepts are unafraid to admit when they have made a mistake, and they actually learn from those errors. They are secure in who they are, what they have learned, and where they are headed down their own spiritual path. Adepts are always open to the discovery of new spiritual lessons.

These lessons can be found within the most everyday of situations and basic of magickal theories. It simply depends on the individual's willingness to get in there and learn.

Witchcraft is a mystery tradition. To truly comprehend it, you must look within and know that those answers have always been right in your own backyard, so to speak. Spirit has been waiting for you to wake up and to pay attention so that you may bring its inspiration, creativity, and purpose into your life and into your craft. The only way to understand this part of the mystery is to live it. There is no one who can do this for you; you must come to understand and to discover this fact about Witchcraft all on your own.

Now that you have been walking this path of the natural Witch for a time, take a careful look around and realize just how far you have traveled. Remember when you first pulled aside those draping branches and discovered this quieter but well-worn path at the beginning of this book? Think of how far you have come, and now look to the future and see how much more of this pathway lies ahead, unexplored and waiting for you. For no matter how wise you are, there will always be more to learn. And the next spiritual lesson is waiting just beyond the horizon.

As was stated in the opening pages, one of the most important mysteries for you to realize is that true magick comes from within. Embrace all of the ways that magick manifests into your existence—on the intuitive, the personal, and the practical levels. Become inspired by and thankful for the sacred things in your life each and every day. Allow the element of spirit to rekindle the flames of knowledge, then learn from the many lessons your life brings you, for this is how we gain wisdom, and it is a type of magickal self-empowerment that sparks deep inside you, within the soul.

May you walk your chosen path wisely,

May your heart with love overflow.

Let your intuition guide you safely,

Feel the magick that around you grows.

For knowledge in time becomes wisdom,

And enlightenment is within your grasp.

Pass it along to your daughters and sons,

And make the natural witchery truly last.

If you practice an art, be proud of it
and make it proud of you . . .

Maxwell Anderson

Book of Witchery

Adding this Book of Witchery was something I simply couldn't resist. Over the past few years, I have had many requests to put all "the good stuff" in one spot so readers could thumb through it and pull out the specific magickal correspondence information that they needed when it came time to create spells of their own design. As a practical Witch, this made good sense to me.

Now, please keep in mind that this is a basic list, but all the supplies and information are easy to understand and, better yet, easy to acquire. This Book of Witchery starts out with magickal correspondences for the days of the week. You will also find information on the magick of colors, crystals, stones, herbs, and flowers, plus there are new Witchcraft projects, such as herbal wreaths and creating herbal candles, for you to try your hand at. There are also a few spells and charms for enchanting those various Craft projects. Finally, you'll find rhyming quarter calls, circlecastings, and a spell worksheet. So peruse this Book of Witchery, jot down your own notes on the blank pages, and make it uniquely your own. Most of all, just enjoy it!

DAILY CORRESPONDENCES

The Bewitching Days of the Week

SUNDAY—Corresponds to the sun. Colors: yellow and gold. Work magick for success, new projects, the sun god.

MONDAY—Corresponds to the moon. Colors: white and silver. Work magick for women's mysteries, psychic abilities, dreams, travel, and the Goddess.

TUESDAY—Corresponds to the planet Mars. Colors: red and black. Work magick for passion, fighting for what you believe in, courage, and defense.

WEDNESDAY—Corresponds to the planet Mercury. Colors: orange and purple. Work magick for communication, cleverness, creativity, and speed.

THURSDAY—Corresponds to the planet Jupiter. Colors: green and royal blue. Work magick for prosperity, abundance, leadership, and healing.

FRIDAY—Corresponds to the planet Venus. Colors: pink and aqua. Work magick for love, romance, beauty, and fertility.

SATURDAY—Corresponds to the planet Saturn. Colors: black and dark purple. Work magick for banishings, bindings, and protection.

• • •

_____

_____

_____

_____

As merry as the day is long.

SHAKESPEARE

_____

_____

_____

_____

_____

_____

_____

_____

_____

_____

_____

_____

_____

_____

_____

CONJURING WITH COLOR AND LIGHT

Color and Candle Magick

This correspondence list may be used for candle or for color magick. So if you are whipping up a charm bag for an enchanting herbal sachet or simply choosing a candle for a quick candle spell, here is a guide to the colors and their magickal definitions.

PINK—Affection, friendship, warm fuzzies, and children's magick.

RED—Love, passion, courage, the element of fire, and the Mother Goddess.

ORANGE—Energy, vitality, harvest, and intensity.

YELLOW—Creativity, communication, knowledge, and the element of air.

GREEN—Prosperity, health, gardening, herbalism, faerie magick, the earth element, and the Green Man or god of nature.

BLUE—Peace, hope, healing, and the element of water.

PURPLE—Psychic powers, spirituality, to increase personal power, and faerie magick.

BROWN—Homes, pets, and garden magick.

BLACK—Protection, breaking hexes, banishing illness and negativity, and the Crone Goddess.

WHITE—All-purpose color, peace, calm, hope, and the Maiden Goddess.

GREY—Bindings, neutrality, invisibility spells, and glamours.

SILVER—The Goddess, women's mysteries, and the moon.

GOLD—The God, success, wealth, fame, and the sun.

• • •

But I *see your true colors shining through*

I see your true colors and that's why I love you.

So don't be afraid to let them show

Your true colors, true colors

are beautiful like a rainbow.

BILL STEINBERG AND TOM KELLY

PRACTICAL CANDLE MAGICK

Tips, Tricks, and Creative Ideas

Spell candles come in all shapes and sizes. You may use tapers, votives, tealights, pillars, or those mini-spell candles that are so popular in magickal shops these days. While burning candles, you will need the appropriate holder for obvious safety and neatness reasons.

Tapers come in many lengths and will require candlesticks. They can be whatever style you prefer and may be made out of whatever nonflammable material you like, such as ceramic, glass, or metal. Votives require a votive cup, since they have a very high oil content and will turn to liquid wax right away. If you do not burn the votive inside of a votive cup, you are going to have a huge mess on your altar.

A tealight is already contained inside of a little metal cup, but the metal does heat up so you will have to put it somewhere heatproof. (I use a little miniature metal cauldron when I burn my tealights—found it on a Halloween endcap display one year and thought it made a great, witchy tealight holder; a tealight fits inside of it perfectly.) Oh, and lest we forget: those mini tapers that come in a rainbow of colors and are so popular will need a special mini holder, too. You will find them right next to the mini taper displays. I have a few: a blue glass holder shaped like a star and a simple white ceramic mini taper holder with a crescent moon on it.

If you choose to work with pillar or glass jar candles, you will also need to think about fire safety. If I am burning a pillar candle or a glass jar seven-day candle, I usually tuck them inside a large metal cauldron and then set that on top of my cast-iron wood-burning stove. Since the candle will burn around the clock for several days—if the glass

_____

_____

_____

_____

_____

_____

_____

_____

_____

_____   *Colors seen by candlelight*

_____   *will not look the same by day.*

_____   ELIZABETH BARRETT BROWNING

_____

_____

_____

_____

_____

_____

_____

_____

should crack or a cat would decide to try and nudge against it, the jar candle or pillar will stay contained within a fireproof area.

Here is a crafty idea for an inexpensive holder for a pillar candle: paint small clay saucers. Check out the flowerpot section of the local craft store and snag a few terra-cotta saucers. I have a set of four-inch terra-cotta saucers that I have painted for my quarter candles, one in each elemental color, and they also come in very handy as decorative holders for my quarter candles.

You could take this idea even further and paint up a few saucers for lunar magick, protection magick, and so on. Decorate the saucers with runic symbols or other magickal symbols that are meaningful to you, such as pentagrams or elemental symbols. I recommend using nontoxic acrylic craft paint, or try the decorative paint pens made especially for clay pots.

Lighting the Candles and to Snuff, to Pinch, or to Blow Out . . . That Is the Question

Now, when it comes to actually lighting the candles, for candle magick you can either light the candles with a match or use a lighter; either technique is fine. Some folks hate the smell of sulfur or are nervous around stick matches. I usually use butane lighters, since they are handy and quick. I have been to many a circle or group ritual where the "ceremonial lighter" is passed around from person to person so each of the folks standing at the quarters can easily light the quarter candles. It is practical and convenient.

_____

_____

_____

_____

_____

_____

_____

_____

_____

_____

_____

_____

_____

_____

_____

_____

_____

_____

_____

_____

_____

Said the Wind to the Moon,

"I will blow you out!"

George MacDonald

Many of us don't worry about extinguishing spell candles—we usually tend to let those burn until they go out on their own, with the thought that the spell candle will only be used that one time. However, in the case of illuminator or quarter candles, you do pinch, snuff, or blow them out, because you will be using them again.

Now, I have read the debates and heard people screech about how "disrespectful" it is to blow out a magickal candle. But if you have to put out quarter candles and somebody forgot to bring along the snuffer into the circle or is afraid to pinch out the flame, you may not have any choice in the matter. (I personally hate to pinch out candles—I always get burned. Don't bother giving me tips on how to do it. I always wimp out and get nervous, then scorch my witchy fingers.)

Truthfully, the sky will not fall in. I'd hate to imagine you running around the circle like Chicken Little, in a panic because you are worried about offending the gods by blowing out a quarter candle. Be practical, and do what works best for you. It is really going to blow the mood of your spell or ritual if you have to stop everything to go on the hunt for the candle snuffer.

• • •

Scents and Oils

Essential Oils and Their Magickal Properties

In chapter 4 there were seasonal spells featured that all employed essential oils and those practical little oil-burner lamps. If you liked that idea and would like to craft a few of your own personalized spells, here is a short list of common essential oils, their magickal uses, and their planetary and elemental properties as well.

Remember: not all essential oil is suitable for direct contact with the skin. Some may cause blistering or an allergic reaction.

BERGAMOT—Aligned to Mercury and the element of air. It promotes energy and success.

CINNAMON—Corresponds to the sun and to the element of fire. This oil brings prosperity and energy, and increases your psychic responses.

CLOVES—Planetary influence is Jupiter. Elemental correspondence is fire. This is a good oil for protection, courage, and power.

EUCALYPTUS—Aligned with the planet Mercury and the element of air. It is used for healing purification.

FRANKINCENSE—Corresponds to the sun and the element of air. This is the oil for spirituality and meditation, and it also helps to relieve stress.

HONEYSUCKLE—Aligned to Jupiter and the earth element. This oil is a good one for prosperity, and it also boosts your psychic and intuitive abilities.

JASMINE—Associated with the moon and the element of water. This is a good fragrance for keeping your intuitive powers working at their highest levels. It is also used to promote sensuality, love, peace, and spirituality.

Lavender's blue,
dilly dilly,
lavender's green …
Nursery Rhyme

LAVENDER—Aligned to Mercury and the element of air. A wonderful oil for calming nerves, healing, cleansing, and for removing stress and anxiety.

NEROLI—Corresponds to the sun and to fire. This oil imparts joy, happiness, and energy.

OAKMOSS—Corresponds with Jupiter and the element of earth. This earthy oil encourages bounty and thankfulness, and it helps to get your personal prosperity up and running.

PATCHOULI—Corresponds with the planetary influence of Saturn and the element of earth. This oil is a sexual stimulant, and its earthy scent brings prosperity.

ROSE—Corresponds to Venus and the element of water. This oil is for love and compassion, promoting inner beauty and, of course, sexuality.

ROSEMARY—Associated with the sun and the element of fire, it improves memory and helps to bring about positive change.

SANDALWOOD—Aligned with the moon and the element of water. A mystical, all-purpose magickal oil. A staple in most Witches' magickal cabinets.

YLANG-YLANG—Corresponds with the moon and the element of water. This oil promotes happiness, increases desire, and encourages love.

• • •

_____

_____

_____

_____

_____

_____

_____

_____

_____

_____

_____

_____

_____

_____

_____

_____

_____

_____

_____

_____

_____

What's in a name?

That which we call a rose

By any other name would smell as sweet.

SHAKESPEARE

A Witch's Dozen of Crystals & Stones

Crystal and stone magick is one of those basics that many Witches begin with. Almost every Witch I know has a small bowl or bag full of tumbled stones that they keep on hand for charms and spells. Here are thirteen of my favorites, and the best part is that these crystals and tumbled stones are typically easy to find in metaphysical or magickal shops. They are also relatively inexpensive to purchase.

Amber—This resin promotes healing, beauty, and strength. (Amber and jet beads are often worn together by high priests and priestesses to denote their rank.)

Amethyst—Calming, healing, and centering.

Aventurine—Good luck and prosperity; draws cash.

Bloodstone—Healing and protection.

Carnelian—Passion and energy.

Hematite—Protection and grounding; helps remove migraines.

Jet—Grants power over troublesome situations and individuals.

Lapis Lazuli—Healing stone sacred to Isis.

Moonstone—Safe travel, moon magick, and psychic abilities.

Obsidian—Protection and destressing.

Quartz Crystal—Boosts your own power and any other stone it is with.

Rose Quartz—The "warm fuzzy" stone; love, friendship, and compassion.

Tiger's-Eye—Protection and energy.

• • •

_____

_____

_____

_____   *Magic and stones are anciently related.*

_____   SCOTT CUNNINGHAM

_____

_____

_____

_____

_____

_____

_____

_____

_____

_____

_____

_____

WORKING WITH STONE & CRYSTAL MAGICK

Stones, crystals, minerals, and semiprecious and precious gems are natural gifts from the element of earth. What better way to tap into magick than by rediscovering their awesome powers and magickal qualities? As they hold and focus the earth's energies, stones, crystals, and gems are magickal batteries of sorts.

There are three important qualities needed for working this type of earth magick, and they are 1) the goal, or magical intention; 2) the desire to create a positive change (getting your affirmative emotions involved so your spell will pack a punch); and 3) the knowledge and basic skill to be able to perform the spell.

So, let's celebrate the beauty, power, and mystery of the treasures of the earth. Listed below is the information that will help you expand your knowledge.

Energies of the Stones: Projective and Receptive

There are two types of energies inherent in crystals, gems, and stones: projective and receptive. Projective energies are sometimes described as electric, hot, day, physical, bright, summer, masculine, and active. Receptive energies are often described as magnetic, cold, night, spiritual, dark, winter, feminine, and inert. It is important to know that one type of energy is not superior to the other, for they each have their place in magick, and they both bring balance to our lives.

Projective stone energies are able to get in touch with the conscious mind. They are associated with the sun and the planets Mercury and Mars. They are also linked to the masculine elements of air and fire. These stones tend to fall in the color range of red, orange, yellow, gold, clear, and sometimes black. They can be utilized to fight disease, and

can attract good luck. Projective stones bring vitality and health, and they also may impart courage and success to their bearers. These projective stones are powerful tools to fight off negativity, boost your physical energy levels, and grant you a strong sense of grit and determination. A few projective stones to try for these purposes are amber, banded and brown agates, carnelian, citrine, garnet, hematite, onyx, quartz crystal points, red agate, red jasper, tiger's-eye, topaz, and zircon.

Receptive stones have the opposite sort of energies. These are associated with the moon and the planets Venus, Saturn, Jupiter, and Neptune. They are associated with the feminine elements of earth and water, and they are often cooler colors, such as green, blue, purple, grey, silver, pink, and black. These receptive stones are wonderful tools for soothing and calming situations and people. They promote grounding, may assist in meditation, and can help folks search within to find the answers they seek.

Receptive stones and crystals can also promote spirituality and wisdom, as they encourage peace and psychic abilities. A few receptive crystals and stones to work with include amethyst, azurite, blue and green agates, chalcedony, green jasper, lapis lazuli, malachite, moonstone, opal, peridot, rose quartz, sapphire, tourmaline (black, blue, green, or pink), and turquoise.

• • •

STONES:
THEIR COLORS & THEIR MAGICKAL MEANINGS

Just like in candle magick, crystals and stones may be grouped together by their colors. Here is a straightforward listing for you to peruse and to work your earth magick with.

RED—Red stones and crystals are definitely projective ones. Typically related to the planet Mars and the element of fire, they are forceful powers. Red stones such as carnelian promote courage and bravery, while red jasper promotes valor and banishes fatigue. Red crystals and gems also give the body a burst of energy, both for athletic prowess or for sex. Red stones may be incorporated into healing rituals and spells. Try these for drawing out the heat of skin irritations or minor burns.

ORANGE—Orange crystals and stones are thought to be a gentler version of red ones. They are also projective and associated with the sun, such as the orange-colored stone citrine, which can grant you a positive outlook on life. These sunny stones and crystals are perfect for shedding some light on a subject or for a little creative illumination. Orange stones are linked to personal power. They can boost your self-confidence and self-esteem. This is a successful color. Work with it to pump up the volume on your own vitality, creativity, and energy.

This precious stone set in the silver sea ...

SHAKESPEARE

YELLOW—Yellow gemstones and crystals are projective. These will fall under the influence of the sun, the planet Mercury, and the element of air. And what a surprise: they are worked into magick for communication, visualization, and perception! These are the stones to work with when you need to get the old brain kicked into high gear. If you need help expressing yourself, whether it's in public speaking or writing, work with yellow stones and crystals. These babies will make you more eloquent while you are speaking and or writing, plus your thoughts will flow more freely.

GREEN—Green stones, gems, and crystals reflect the colors of life, nature, and fruitfulness. Green is a receptive color and may be worked into spells for healing, gardening, grounding, good luck, and prosperity. A mystical green crystal to try is malachite. This stone encourages success, draws cash, and can even protect its bearer from danger. Any green-colored gemstone or crystal may also be incorporated into spells that work with the faerie kingdom or the elementals. As you'd expect, this color of stone is tied to the element of earth.

BLUE—Blue gems and stones are receptive and often linked to the element of water and the planet Neptune. These crystals promote peace and soothing emotions. They can be used to promote a good night's sleep and may keep away bad dreams. A good blue stone to try is the blue lace agate. This stone has all of the qualities listed above. As blue is a healing color, blue stones are often incorporated into healing rituals, charms, and spells.

_____

_____

_____

_____

_____

_____

_____

_____

_____

_____

_____

_____

_____

_____

_____

_____

_____

_____

_____

_____

PURPLE—Purple crystals are receptive and also spiritual. These gems and stones correspond with Jupiter and Neptune. Purple is the color of magick, royalty, and the gods. Purple or violet gemstones such as amethyst promote spirituality, protection, and peace. Purple stones can alleviate tension headaches and help reduce stress and anxiety. Displaying a cluster of amethyst crystal points makes negative energy dissipate, provides balance, and restores harmony in your home.

PINK—Pink stones and crystals are also receptive stones and bring warm, fuzzy feelings. They are linked to the planet Venus and are used to promote love, happiness, and friendships, as well as soothe frayed nerves and tempers. Stones such as the rose quartz can help encourage relaxation of both the mind and the spirit. They also can help end the spat between a feuding couple by magnifying loving feelings and relieving anger. Given as a token between friends, pink stones can gently link one magickal friend to another.

WHITE—White stones and crystals fall in the receptive stone category and are governed by the moon. These stones have the magickal qualities of promoting safe travel, a good night's sleep, psychic abilities, intuition, and, of course, moon magick. White stones such as the moonstone are traditional stones used to open up psychic receptors and to encourage empathy. The moonstone is a popular magickal stone and is often worked into Goddess magick and rituals.

_____

_____

_____

_____

_____

When I am an old woman,

I shall wear purple . . .

JENNY JOSEPH

_____

_____

_____

_____

_____

_____

_____

_____

_____

_____

_____

_____

_____

BLACK—Black stones are also receptive and sometimes projective. As the color black absorbs light, so, too, will a black stone absorb negativity, despair, and anger. These ebony-colored crystals and gems are ruled by the planet Saturn. Black stones are perfect for protection work, for grounding, and for removing negativity. Some black stones, like jet, can actually help you gain influence over obnoxious or difficult people. These stones are talismans for security, self-control, and power.

• • •

_____

_____

_____

_____

_____

_____

_____

_____

_____

_____

_____

_____

_____

_____

_____   *Talk of mysteries!*

_____   *Think of our life in nature—*

_____   *daily to be shown matter, to come in contact*

_____   *with it—rocks, trees, wind on our cheeks!*

_____   HENRY DAVID THOREAU

A Witch's Dozen of Magickal Herbs

Please note: These herbs are listed for their use in spells and charm bags only. Be very careful while working with botanicals. Avoid handling them if you are pregnant or nursing. Some herbs are potentially toxic, and others may cause irritation to sensitive skin.

In this list, you will find the common names for the herb followed by the botanical name in italics. This is to help you identify which witchy herb you are working with. Keep all botanicals out of the reach of small children and pets.

For more detailed information on working with herbs in magick, or for growing them in the magickal garden, please refer to my previous books *Garden Witchery* and *Herb Magic for Beginners*.

BASIL, SWEET BASIL, GARDEN BASIL—(*Ocimum basilicum*) Basil brings compassion and helps end bickering and feuds between two people; an herb of loving vibrations.

DILL—(*Anethum graveolens*) Dill is worked into spells and charms for protection and prosperity.

FEVERFEW—(*Tanacetum parthenium*) This dainty flowering herb brings healing and protection from illness.

GARLIC—(*Allium sativum*) Garlic protects and banishes evil. A rope of garlic hung in the kitchen denotes a kitchen Witch's domain. Helps ward off psychic vampires, too!

HELIOTROPE—(*Heliotropium arborescens*) When this flowering herb is planted in your garden, it helps keep nosey neighbors distracted. This herb classically is used to confer invisibility. (The foliage may cause contact dermatitis.)

_____

_____

_____

_____

_____

_____

There's fennel for you, and columbines;

there's rue for you;

and here's some for me;

we may call it herb of grace o' Sundays.

SHAKESPEARE

_____

_____

_____

_____

_____

_____

_____

_____

_____

_____

_____

_____

MUGWORT—(*Artemisia vulgaris*) Mugwort promotes psychic powers, protection, and prophetic dreams. (Do not ingest, and avoid handling while pregnant.)

PEONY—(*Paeonia officinalis*) This common flowering shrub is, in fact, an herb. The blossoms ward off nightmares; use its flowers in protection magick.

ROSE—(*Rosa* ssp.) The petals of the rose speed up your magick, and the flowers promote love. (Note that the different colors of the rose will each have their own specialties.)

ROSEMARY, DEW OF THE SEA—(*Rosmarinus officinalis*) Rosemary ensures a good night's sleep and is worked into charms for remembrance and love.

RUE—(*Ruta graveolens*) A classic protection magick herb. Rue is toxic and should be kept out of the reach of children and avoided by pregnant women. This herb removes the evil eye, breaks manipulative magick, and is very protective; I think of it as the "hex buster."

THYME, COMMON THYME—(*Thymus vulgaris*) This delicate herb encourages prophetic dreams and psychic abilities.

VALERIAN—(*Valeriana officinalis*) The fragrant flowers are used for protection and to drive away negativity. Tuck it into your gardens to mark the boundaries of a magickal garden, and give it lots of room to flourish.

YARROW, MILFOIL—(*Achillea millefolium*) The wise woman's herb, yarrow is an all-purpose botanical. It's a gorgeous blooming perennial that dries well and is popular for enchanting arts and crafts and flower arranging. This flower is also thought to keep a couple happily married for seven years. (Warning: yarrow may cause contact dermatitis.)

• • •

I know a bank whereon the wild thyme blows ...

SHAKESPEARE

FLOWER FASCINATIONS FROM A–Z

The folklore of flowers is a fascinating subject, and it is simple to work into natural spells and charms. Check out this alphabet of common garden blossoms and see what type of natural magick you can add to your next spell or charm by employing the language of flowers. (For a more detailed listing, please refer to *Garden Witchery*.)

AZALEA—First love, a tender romance.

BEGONIA—A warning. Also, red begonias are traditional protective flowers for windowboxes.

CROCUS—New beginnings, youth, and happiness.

DAISY—Innocence, simplicity, and joy.

ECHINACEA—(Coneflower) Skill and dexterity.

FOXGLOVE—Faerie magick, a wish.

GARDENIA—Charmed, "I love you."

HYDRANGEA—Protection, "hopelessly devoted to you."

IRIS—Messages sacred to the Greco-Roman goddess of the rainbow, Iris.

JONQUIL—Esteem, chivalry, and holding someone in high regard.

KALANCHOE—Fame and personal status.

LILAC—First love, beauty, a faerie favorite.

MORNING GLORY (BLUE)—Protection, and it is sacred to the goddess Venus/ Aphrodite.

_____

_____

_____

_____

_____

Correct handling of flowers refines the personality.

GUSTIE L. HERRIGEL

_____

_____

_____

_____

_____

_____

_____

_____

_____

_____

_____

_____

_____

_____

_____

NIGELLA (LOVE IN A MIST)—Kiss me, a rare love.

ORCHID—Exotic passion, luxury, and love.

PANSY—Ease a broken heart and bring affection and cheer.

QUEEN ANNE'S LACE—Homecoming and shelter.

RANUNCULUS—Bedazzled.

SUNFLOWER—The magick and might of the sun; esteem and riches.

TIGER LILY—Energy and erotic love.

VIOLET—Enchantment and protection against faerie mischief.

WISTERIA—Welcome.

YELLOW ROSE—Friendship and sunshine.

ZINNIA—Friendship.

• • •

_____

_____

_____

_____

_____

_____

_____

The Zinnia's solitary flower,

which blooms in forests lone and deep,

are like the visions fair and bright

that faithful, absent hearts will keep.

FLORA'S INTERPRETER

_____

_____

_____

_____

_____

_____

_____

_____

_____

_____

_____

HERBAL ARTS AND WITCHCRAFT PROJECTS

Making Wreaths

As long as you are warming up the creative side of your brain, consider this: herbal wreaths are magickal craft items that are fun to create. These wreaths may even be incorporated into a variety of spells and charms. This way, you are not only getting your spell-writing juices flowing, you are also creatively working with the herbs at the same time!

Herbal wreaths can serve as a gift or be used as a tool for a specific magickal purpose, such as protection, love, or prosperity. Wreathmaking is an ancient practice. The wreath has been used since the Middle Ages to celebrate the changing seasons and holidays. Creating herbal wreaths is a fun and enjoyable process, and best of all, it's not expensive or hard to do.

There are three basic elements to wreathmaking: the base, the materials used, and the method of attachment. Many of the items you'll need to decorate your wreath may be homegrown or easily located at the local arts and crafts store. Before you go and plunk down lots of money, though, first take a walk around the yard or herb garden. See how you can incorporate the natural bounty that nature has to offer. The herb garden has much to provide to the clever herbalist and Witch. There are gorgeous flowering herbs and magickal flowers, changing autumn leaves, acorns, pine cones, twigs, or even a fallen feather or two. Often a lazy hour spent outdoors yields more organic material than any trip to the store.

When you begin to assemble the components for your own herbal wreaths, you may find it helpful to refer to the herbal correspondence charts listed here on pages 226 and 228. You can really add more magickal punch to this project if you time the creation of

I sent thee late a rosy wreath …

BEN JONSON

your herbal wreath with a certain phase of the moon or day of the week, although don't forget your intuition: let your instincts guide you.

The basic supplies you will need for herbal wreaths are:

- A low-temperature glue gun and glue sticks
- Florist wire, gauge 20
- Floral picks
- A base, such as a 12- to 18-inch grapevine wreath
- Dried or fresh herbs, flowers, seed pods, nuts, and small twigs
- Ribbons in assorted colors and widths
- Small metal celestial charms (optional)

Directions

Gather your material with intention. Refer to the correspondence charts or follow your own instincts. Next, arrange your wreath by laying out the herbal components. Take your time, and position things to your liking. Have fun and relax so you can enjoy yourself. (Remember that it's much easier to shift pieces around before you glue them on than it is to pry them off afterwards.) If you are incorporating twigs or berries, try and work them into the grapevine for a more natural look. After you have chosen the design, then carefully hot-glue or wire the natural material, ribbons, and celestial charms onto the grapevine.

Another great tip that I can pass along to you is if you are working with large clusters of flowers such as yarrow blossoms or roses, then work with an odd number. (This is an old floral designer's tip!) There is something about even numbers that always makes

_____

_____

_____

_____

_____

_____

_____

_____

_____

_____

_____

_____

_____

_____

_____

_____

_____

_____

_____

wreaths look like a clock face. Go for threes and fives for your main flowers. Perhaps you can weave a pentagram in the center of your wreath with the ribbons. Tie on a pretty bow or have ribbon streamers dangling from the bottom. Also, those celestial charms would look great tied to the end of the streamers. Go with whatever you like the best; the possibilities are endless.

An All-Purpose Spell for Herbal Wreaths

Once you have your wreath all arranged and finished, you will want to enchant it. Try this all-purpose spell to activate the magick within your herbal creation. Hold the finished wreath in your hands and transfer a bit of your personal power into the wreath. Then repeat the following verse:

See the magickal herbs arranged on this circle of vine?

These will bring enchantment and blessings to us at all times.

Made with my own two hands, this herbal magick begins.

Now grant us prosperity, happiness, and wisdom.

For the good of all, this herbalist's spell is spun.

As I will, so mote it be, and let it harm none.

When you are finished, ground and center yourself. Hang up your enchanted herbal wreath in a prominent place.

_____

_____

_____

_____

_____

_____

_____

_____

_____

_____

_____

_____

_____

_____

_____

_____

_____

_____

_____

Craft, then, is more than a manual art.

It's a connection with ourselves;

a valuable tool that we can use to alter our lives.

SCOTT CUNNINGHAM & DAVID HARRINGTON

Herbal Beeswax Candles

Have you ever tried your hand at making your own herbal candles? Just think, specialty herbal candles you can create and imbue with your own positive personal power. Then you would have custom-made magickal supplies right at your fingertips. How cool is that? You can make herbal candles for healing, prosperity, affection, or protection.

There is a simple way to do this, and it won't require you to have wax boiling away on the stove, which can be expensive, messy, and dangerous. You will still need to make a trip to the local arts and crafts supply store, however. But the following candle project is a practical, affordable alternative to purchased candles.

Hit the candlemaking aisle, and look for sheets of beeswax and wicks. I have even found beeswax candlemaking kits! You may use colored beeswax sheets or the plain, old-fashioned-looking honey-colored ones. (You may find it helpful to refer back to page 200 for a color/candle magick guide.) So choose your supplies and ingredients, and let's get started!

Candlemaking Supplies and Directions

- Assorted sheets of beeswax (approximately 16 x 8 inches)
- Wicks (look for lead-free wicks)
- A hair dryer
- Assorted magickal herbs

All nature seems at work.

Slugs leave their lair—the bees are stirring—

birds are on the wing—

SAMUEL TAYLOR COLERIDGE

How to Make Rolled Herbal Candles

1. If the beeswax you are working with is rolled, then gently unroll it. (If it is hard, stiff, or might crack while unrolling, then soften it up by warming it with the hair dryer set on low.)

2. Lay a piece of wick along one of the short edges of the beeswax sheet. Warm the beeswax up with the hair dryer set on the lowest setting.

3. Sprinkle the sheet with your chosen magickal herb. Gently press the herbs down into the sheet of wax.

4. Finally, carefully roll it up. Your herbs will stay between the layers as you roll the candle. (Think of a jellyroll type of situation.)

5. When you have finished rolling all the wax, run the hair dryer over the candle again. This molds the edges together just a bit and softens the bottom so that you can give the candle a nice, flat, smooth surface.

A Charm to Enchant Your Herbal Candles

To enchant your handmade herbal candle, try this quick charm. Hold the herbal candle in your hands, and repeat the following:

Goddess, bless this herb candle made by my own hands,

May it spread enchantment and light across the land.

• • •

CIRCLE MECHANICS

Quarter Calls and a Circlecasting

Here is one of my favorite quarter calls and circlecastings. I like this one the best as the quarter calls rhyme and are simple and uncomplicated. Plus it was very easy for me to commit it to memory. Typically, I begin my quarter calls in the east, which is the direction that I associate with the air element. Your own magickal traditions may be different. Some practitioners may begin their quarter calls in the north or have different quarter associations for air and fire—and if that is the case, then I invite you to rework this to suit your own practice.

Begin by moving to the eastern quarter. Light the yellow quarter candle, and say:

In the eastern quarter,

I call knowledge and intuition true.

Move to your right, and go to the southern quarter. Light the red quarter candle, and say:

At the southern quarter,

I call for passion and courage in all that I do.

Turn to your right again, and go to the western quarter. Light the blue quarter candle, and say:

Here in the west,

grant me visions and bless me with love.

'Tis now the very witching
time of night.

SHAKESPEARE

Finally, move to your right, and go to the northern quarter. Light the green quarter candle, and say:

In the north,

I call for security and strength from the gods above.

Now move to the center of the circle, and bind or seal the circle. Turn in a clockwise (deosil) motion, and spin slowly around, casting the circle by pointing at the ground and saying:

As above, now so below; the elemental powers spin, and my magick holds.

After your ritual, spellwork, or celebration is complete, you may open the circle in the following manner: this time, we begin in the northern quarter. Turning to the left and working in a counterclockwise (widdershins) direction, go to the west, then the south, and then finally end in the east. I typically say at each quarter,

Hail and farewell to the element of the [earth, water, etc.]; many thanks, blessed be.

Keep in mind that you will switch out the word in brackets to suit each quarter, so in this case it would be opening the quarters in the order of earth, water, fire, and air.

After you have worked your way completely around the circle, move to the center, and say:

The circle is now open but unbroken;

Release the magick as my words are spoken.

• • •

[T]he power of the world always works in circles,

and everything tries to be round.

<small>BLACK ELK</small>

Spell Worksheet

Goal:

Moon Phase:

Day of the Week:

Astrological/ Magickal Symbols Used:

Candle Color (if you added candle magick):

Herbs Used:

Magickal Significance of the Herbs:

Crystals or Stones Used and Their Associations:

Charm or verse:

Results:

Now comes the end of the book;
Many blessings on your spells and charms.
May you walk your chosen path wisely,
And never cause any harm.

It is the supreme art of the teacher to awaken joy in

creative expression and knowledge.

ALBERT EINSTEIN

Bibliography

Andrews, Ted. *Animal-Speak*. St. Paul, MN: Llewellyn, 1994.

———. *How to Develop and Use Psychometry*. St. Paul, MN: Llewellyn, 1994.

Ban Breathnach, Sarah. *Simple Abundance: A Daybook of Comfort and Joy*. New York, NY: Warner Books, 1995.

Bartlett's Familiar Quotations. Ed. John Bartlett. Boston, MA: Little, Brown and Company, 1992.

Beth, Rae. *The Wiccan Way: Magical Spirituality for the Solitary Pagan*. Blaine, WA: Phoenix Publishing, 2001.

Biziou, Barbara. *The Joy of Ritual*. New York, NY: Golden Books, 1999.

Budapest, Zsuzsanna. *The Goddess in the Office*. San Francisco, CA: HarperSan-Francisco, 1993.

Burns, Litany. *Develop Your Psychic Abilities*. New York, NY: Pocket Books, 1985.

Cabot, Laurie, and Tom Cowan. *Power of the Witch*. New York, NY: Delta Books, 1989.

Crowley, Vivianne. *The Magickal Life*. New York, NY: Penguin Compass, 2003.

Cunningham, Scott. *Magical Aromatherapy*. St. Paul, MN: Llewellyn, 1993.

———. *Cunningham's Encyclopedia of Wicca in the Kitchen*. St. Paul, MN: Llewellyn, 2005.

———. *Cunningham's Encyclopedia of Crystal, Gem, & Metal Magic*. St. Paul, MN: Llewellyn, 1992.

Curott, Phyllis. *Book of Shadows*. New York, NY: Broadway Books, 1998.

———. *The Love Spell*. New York, NY: Gotham Books, 2005.

Dolnick, Barrie. *The Executive Mystic: Psychic Power Tools for Success*. New York, NY: Harper Collins, 1998.

———. *Simple Spells for Success*. New York, NY: Harmony Books, 1996.

Dugan, Ellen. *7 Days of Magic: Spells, Charms & Correspondences for the Bewitching Week*. St. Paul, MN: Llewellyn, 2004.

———. *Cottage Witchery : Natural Magick for Hearth and Home*. St. Paul, MN: Llewellyn, 2005.

———. *Elements of Witchcraft: Natural Magick for Teens*. St. Paul, MN: Llewellyn, 2003.

———. *Garden Witchery: Magick from the Ground Up*. St. Paul, MN: Llewellyn, 2003.

———. "Full Moon Rituals." *Witches' Datebook 2007*. Woodbury, MN: Llewellyn, 2006.

———. "Earth Magic." *Magical Almanac 2007*. Woodbury, MN: Llewellyn, 2006.

Einstein, Patricia. *Intuition: The Path to Inner Wisdom*. Rockport, MA: Element Books, 1997.

Fortune, Dion. *Applied Magic*, first ed. London: The Aquarian Publishing Company, 1962.

Gallagher, Ann-Marie. *The Spells Bible*. Cincinnati, OH: Walking Stick Press, 2003.

Grimassi, Raven. *Encyclopedia of Wicca & Witchcraft*. St. Paul, MN: Llewellyn, 2000.

———. *The Wiccan Mysteries: Ancient Origins & Teachings*. St. Paul, MN: Llewellyn, 1997.

Hall, Judy. *Principles of Psychic Protection*. Hammersmith, London, UK: Thorsons, 1999.

Inner Knowing: Consciousness, Creativity, Insight and Intuition. Ed. Helen Palmer. New York, NY: Jeremy P. Tarcher/Putnam, 1998.

Johnson, Julie Tallard. *Teen Psychic: Exploring Your Intuitive Spiritual Powers*. Rochester, VT: Bindu Books, 2003.

Laufer, Geraldine Adamich. *Tussie-Mussies: The Victorian Art of Expressing Yourself in the Language of Flowers*. New York, NY: Workman Publishing Company, 1993.

Lipp, Deborah. *The Way of Four*. St. Paul, MN: Llewellyn, 2004.

Manning, Al G. *Helping Yourself with White Witchcraft*. West Nyack, NY: Parker Publishing Company, 1972.

Matthews, Caitlin. *Celtic Devotional: Daily Prayers and Blessings*. New York, NY: Harmony Books, 1996.

McCoy, Edain. *Advanced Witchcraft*. St. Paul, MN: Llewellyn, 2004.

Moore, Patrick. *On the Moon*. London: Cassell & Co., 2001.

Penczak, Christopher. *The Inner Temple of Witchcraft*. St. Paul, MN: Llewellyn, 2002.

———. *The Outer Temple of Witchcraft*. St. Paul, MN: Llewellyn, 2004.

Sanders, Pete A. *You Are Psychic*. New York, NY: Ballantine Books, 1989.

Starhawk. *The Spiral Dance*, tenth anniversary ed. San Francisco, CA: Harper Collins, 1989.

Steel, Duncan. *Eclipse: The Celestial Phenomenon That Changed the Course of History*. Washington, DC: Joseph Henry Press, 2001.

Telesco, Patricia. *How to Be a Wicked Witch*. New York, NY: Fireside Books, 2001.

Valiente, Doreen. *Natural Magic*. Custer, WA: Phoenix Publishing, Inc., 1975.

Wolf, Stacey. *Get Psychic! Discover Your Hidden Powers*. New York, NY: Warner Books, 2001.

Websites

www.bartleby.com (miscellaneous quotes accessed July 2005)

www.wikipedia.com (solar eclipse and lunar eclipse accessed October 2005; Andre Danjon accessed May 2006)

http://sunearth.gsfc.nasa.gov/eclipse/eclipse.html (NASA Eclipse Homepage accessed October 2005)

http://www.ynhh.org/online/nutrition/advisor/chocolate.html (accessed February 2006)

Index

GARDEN WITCHERY
Magick from the Ground Up
(Includes a Gardening Journal)

Ellen Dugan

How Does Your Magickal Garden Grow?

Garden Witchery is more than belladonna and wolfsbane. It's about making your own enchanted backyard with the trees, flowers, and plants found growing around you. It's about creating your own flower fascinations and spells, and it's full of common-sense information about cold hardiness zones, soil requirements, and a realistic listing of accessible magickal plants.

There may be other books on magickal gardening, but none have practical gardening advice, magickal correspondences, flower folklore, moon gardening, faerie magick, advanced Witchcraft, and humorous personal anecdotes all rolled into one volume.

0-7387-0318-4
272 pp., 7.5 x 7.5 $17.95

COTTAGE WITCHERY
Natural Magick for Hearth and Home

Ellen Dugan

There's No Place Like A Magickal Home

Ellen Dugan, the author of *Garden Witchery*, is the ideal guide to show us how to bring the beauty of nature and its magickal energies indoors. Using common household and outdoor items—such as herbs, spices, dried flowers, plants, stones, and candles—she offers a down-to-earth approach to creating an enchanted home.

From specialized spells and charms to kitchen conjuring and color magick, this hands-on guide teaches Witches of all levels how to strengthen a home's aura and energy. Readers will learn how to use begonias and lilacs for protection, dispel bad vibes with salt and lemon, perform tea leaf readings, bless the home with fruit, invite the help of faeries, perform houseplant magick, and create a loving home for the whole family.

0-7387-0625-6
288 pp., 7.5 x 7.5 $17.95

To Write to the Author

If you wish to contact the author or would like more information about this book, please write to the author in care of Llewellyn Worldwide and we will forward your request. Both the author and publisher appreciate hearing from you and learning of your enjoyment of this book and how it has helped you. Llewellyn Worldwide cannot guarantee that every letter written to the author can be answered, but all will be forwarded. Please write to:

Ellen Dugan
℅ Llewellyn Worldwide
2143 Wooddale Drive
Woodbury, MN 55125-2989

Please enclose a self-addressed stamped envelope for reply,
or $1.00 to cover costs. If outside U.S.A., enclose
international postal reply coupon.

Many of Llewellyn's authors have websites with additional information and resources. For more information, please visit our website:

HTTP://WWW.LLEWELLYN.COM